Cinema of Choice

Cinema of Choice

Optional Thinking and Narrative Movies

Nitzan Ben Shaul

berghahn
NEW YORK · OXFORD
www.berghahnbooks.com

First edition published in 2012 by
Berghahn Books
www.berghahnbooks.com

© 2012, 2015 Nitzan Ben Shaul
First paperback edition published in 2015

Library of Congress Cataloging-in-Publication Data

Ben Shaul, Nitzan S. Cinema of choice : optional thinking and narrative movies
/ Nitzan Ben Shaul. – 1st ed.
p. cm. Includes bibliographical references and index. Includes filmography.
ISBN 978-0-85745-591-8 (hardback : alk. paper) – ISBN 978-1-78238-904-0
(paperback : alk. paper) – ISBN 978-0-85745-592-5 (ebook)
1. Motion pictures–Philosophy. 2. Motion picture audiences–Psychology. 3.
Motion pictures–Psychological aspects. I. Title.
PN1995.B3445 2012
791.4301–dc23

British Library Cataloguing in Publication Data

A catalogue record for this book is available from the British Library

Printed on acid-free paper.

ISBN 978-0-85745-591-8 (hardback)
ISBN 978-1-78238-904-0 (paperback)
ISBN 978-0-85745-592-5 (ebook)

Contents

Acknowledgments

I am particularly grateful to the anonymous reviewers of the book and to Berghahn editor Mark Stanton, who immediately found the book's theme worthy, offered excellent comments throughout the revision process, and pushed me to expand my discussion of the concept of optional thinking beyond my original intention.

I also thank my wife Daphna for her capacity for optional thinking, her comments throughout the writing process, and her constant encouragement. Our forking and converging life story inspired this book.

1

Introduction

1.1. Optional Thinking and Closed Mindedness

I became concerned with the concept of viable optional thinking after watching *Sliding Doors* (Peter Howitt 1998). In the film we see two parallel, intertwined versions of the life of Helen Quilley (Gwyneth Paltrow) that diverge at a point where she misses or boards the same train as James (John Hannah), a man she has just met. As I was driving home after the movie, I reached a traffic light and asked myself what would happen if instead of taking the usual right turn at the corner I turned left? Though I never actually took that left turn, the thought of possible and viable alternatives filled my mind until I got home. I then realized that this pleasurable cognitive and creative process, that I came to call "optional thinking," rarely occurs during or after watching most movies.

Movies usually tell a story that leads to closure and this does not evoke optional thinking. In fact, most films encourage a closed state of mind, biasing our cognitive processes toward a reductive and selective attention to incoming data. Just recently, I experienced this cognitive bias when I went to a midnight screening of *Harry Brown* (Daniel Barber 2009). In this dark movie, an old man (Michael Caine) takes vengeance on several young delinquents who have

killed his friend and terrorized the inhabitants of his poor neigh-
borhood. After the screening and under the spell of the movie's
dark narrative, I rushed to my car but could not find it. Avoiding
suspicious-looking characters, I hurriedly walked amidst the empty,
dimly lit streets to the nearby police station to report the theft. The
officer on duty took my statement, informed me that there had
been several car thefts in the area and called a cab for me. The next
morning, as I was dialing my insurance agent, it suddenly occurred
to me that I might have parked the car elsewhere. Indeed, I found
my car parked one street down from where I was sure I had left it.
Cognitively and affectively biased by the movie's theme and atmo-
sphere, I had immediately jumped to the conclusion that the car
must have been stolen.

I have been concerned ever since with the affective and cognitive
power of movies on viewers, the tendency of some popular films to
encourage a closed state of mind, and the capacity of some movies
to encourage optional thinking.

"Optional thinking" is used here to refer to the cognitive ability
to generate, perceive, or compare and assess alternative hypotheses
that offer explanations for real or lifelike events. It forms part of
the way we think and acquire and construct knowledge. There is
evidence that not deploying the cognitive ability to generate optional or alternative hypotheses in real-life situations can lead to
premature acceptance of inadequate or incorrect hypotheses that
may result in dire consequences (e.g., Garst et al. 2002). Moreover,
this ability is favorably viewed in cognitive psychological research,
which holds that it indicates "cognitive complexity" (e.g., Burleson
and Kaplan 1998), "critical thinking" (Jones et al. 1995; Paul et al.
1997; Perry 1999), or aptitude for "problem solving" (e.g., Mayer
1992; Newel and Simon 1972) and "decision making" (e.g., Kahneman and Tversky 2000; Triantaphyllou 2000). Its opposite is the
notion of "closed mindedness" (Kruglanski 2004).

While the notion of optional thinking, including its desir-
ability and strategies for its stimulation, is widespread in current
psychological research, I found only one use and definition of the
concept that squarely fits mine. I refer to Platt and Spivack's "Op-

tional Thinking Test," which consists of tasks that "require the subject to conceptualize options to hypothetical but typical real-life problems" (Platt and Spivack 1977: 17).[1] In the test they devised, subjects were given a description of a problem similar to one that might be encountered in real life and asked to offer as many alternative solutions as they could. For example: "John wants to watch his favorite TV program but his friend is watching another program. What can John do so he can have a turn watching TV?" (e.g., push his friend over, persuade him, or bribe him). Then the researchers scored the results according to the quantity of alternatives offered and their degree of relevance to the solution of the problem (e.g., "John could go to a movie" is irrelevant since it avoids the problem). They also considered options offered by subjects that were irrelevant altogether, such as accidental solutions (e.g., "the friend will probably change his mind"). This test was accompanied by two subtests, termed "The Awareness of Consequences Test" and "The Causal Thinking Test," that require subjects to invent little stories leading up to the problem and following it. In these tests the researchers considered whether the part of the story preceding the problem was causally linked to it and whether the portion following the problem resolution took into account relevant consequences. Taken together, these three tests cover the concept of optional thinking discussed in this book by assessing the ability of subjects to construe, entertain, and compare alternate causal narrative chains that converge upon or digress from a shared event.

Rather than dealing with alternate thoughts that occur during mental rumination, free-flowing association, or decontextualized generation of options, I am interested in optional thinking insofar as it forms an integral part of the way we acquire and construct knowledge about the world. It differs from the artistic notion of "open mindedness", as it emphasizes the ability to view things from a fresh or unconventional perspective on account of the causal processing required for knowledge construction. While different "art as opening the mind" approaches claim that art encourages something akin to optional thinking (e.g., Dorn 1999; Eisner 1998; Geahigan 1997; Lampert 2006; Perkins 1994; Stout 1999; Winner and Hetland

2001), they underplay the critical notion of causality (e.g., Lampert 2006: 224). In fact, some research shows that students with high arts exposure are prone to entertain multiple or alternative vantage points but do not tend to consolidate this predisposition into the causal networks characteristic of higher-order thinking (Burton et al. 1999: 43). Often, the "open mind" approach even dismantles causality as a strategy for "opening" a mind perceived as chained by causality. While this approach may be useful in encouraging a predisposition for free-flowing associations, it has little to offer in terms of optional thinking as a causal process of knowledge construction. When viewed from the optional thinking perspective, the disregard or dismantling of causality often inhering in such an approach encourages split attention, confusion, or distraction.[2]

While Spivack and Platt offer an effective test to detect and quantify a person's proficiency in generating alternate hypotheses in respect of situations that replicate those found in real life, the frameworks used to explain this capability or lack thereof are devoid of a comprehensive or generalized theory of motivations, using a different framework for adolescents (Platt and Spivack 1977), deliberate self-harm patients (McAuliffe et al. 2008), or youth at risk (e.g., Benard 1991; Ungar 2001). This content-bound approach is important, particularly in personal and social psychology, but it also implies a problem for someone trying to explain optional thinking proficiency in normal film viewers, for example. Other tests used to evaluate the capability to generate alternate hypotheses, particularly those dealing with problem-solving aptitudes (e.g., Mayer 1992; Newel and Simon 1972), suffer from the inverse problem of detached abstraction. Although the problem-solving approach also focuses on alternative causal reasoning chains, it is usually game-like in that it frames the problem to be solved within a closed and circular set of causally strict alternatives. This "mind-training laboratory" type of approach is somewhat irrelevant to real-life problems. This is because it disregards emotional affects that often bias the knowledge construction process (D'Zurilla and Nezu 1982; Rath et al. 2004) and narrows the subject's awareness of the array of invariables inhering in real-life situations.[3] The abstraction inhering in most problem-solving approaches leads to a pragmatic reduction of different subjects to a common denominator which is not useful for explaining their different motivational factors or their aptitudes for optional thinking in real-life situations.

I therefore offer an approach that brings to bear, upon the process of film viewing, Kruglanski's well researched, empirically corroborated and fruitful theory of a lay epistemic process of knowledge construction and acquisition (e.g., Kruglanski 1980; 1988; 2004). His approach offers a theory that correlates a cognitive process of knowledge acquisition with a theory of epistemic motivation that allows for studying different, specific, content-bound cases without losing sight of their motivational specificity, or of the general principles guiding the knowledge construction process. In a detailed analysis of various cognitive social-psychological theories, Kruglanski shows how his approach integrates content-bound and abstract cognitive-process approaches that have rendered incompatible explanations to the same phenomenon. This is the case, for example, with the ongoing dichotomy between the "cold" and "hot" cognition camps: the former value generalized cognitive processes without taking serious account of how they are biased by epistemic motivations, whereas the latter value epistemic motivations over the general rules of information processing. This cold–hot dichotomy can be evidenced in the cognitive psychological study of film, where cold theories (e.g., Bordwell 1985; N. Carroll 1985) underplay the role of emotion in biasing the cognitive process of knowledge acquisition, whereas hot theories dealing with how films elicit emotional responses in viewers (e.g., Grodal 2009; M. Smith 1995; G.M. Smith 2004; Tan 1996) underplay the rules of cognitive information processing.

David Bordwell's cold theory, for example, while presupposing that the viewers' epistemic motivation to seek knowledge on a given film is directed by their goal to construe in their mind a story and a world out of the movie, does not take into account how cognitive affects cued by a film may heighten the viewers' need to reach their goal on account of the orderly cognitive processing of the information presented before them. This dismissal of cognitive affects results in

Bordwell's mistaken assumption that viewers actively and constantly raise hypotheses concerning what is ahead in the movie rather than being mostly in a state of expectancy toward what awaits them. On the other hand, Ed Tan's hot theory of emotions, for example, in presupposing that emotions force cognition to selectively and exclusively focus upon the emotional concern of the viewer, underestimates the general rules of cognitive information processing as these pertain to the generation of alternative hypotheses and their consequent validation. His approach results in the heralding of the reduction of cognitive activities of viewers of most movies, perceiving this reductionism as a necessary correlate to the movies' valued emotional power.[4]

Kruglanski's approach "recognizes that all information processing is motivated and all motivational influences on the cognitive process operate in informational contexts and are governed by rules of information-processing" (1988: 136). In his "lay epistemic process" of knowledge construction and acquisition (e.g., Kruglanski 1980) he maintains that when lay people are motivated to make a judgment, form an impression, or reach a goal, they usually generate a number of alternative hypotheses to account for the data encountered, and proceed to validate these using further evidence and according to the hypotheses' causal consistency with previously constructed knowledge. Kruglanski then correlates this process of knowledge construction to a generalized matrix of epistemic motivations instigating and accompanying the process, or cued by cognitive affects that arouse them. He subsumes epistemic motivations into four types classifiable on two orthogonal dimensions. The first dimension consists of an epistemic motivation spanning a continuum from a strong need to seek closure to a strong need to avoid it. The second dimension spans from a strong need to seek or avoid closure in respect of a specific kind of content to a strong need for any closure or its avoidance, irrespective of any specific content.

For example, the motivation for closure that is nonspecific may guide a judge who needs to reach a verdict on someone accused of a traffic violation in order to be able to deal with a large amount of cases awaiting him. Rather than seeking a specific verdict (e.g., guilty), this judge needs to quickly reach any verdict and may be content with a review of available data rather than embarking upon a lengthy investigation. In such a case, the judge's motivation for closure reduces the number of hypotheses he raises or compares to reach a conclusion. Conversely, the same judge, when submitting a verdict on someone accused of murder, may be motivated to avoid closure as long as possible since a wrong though nonspecific verdict (guilty or not) carries heavy consequences. In such a case, the judge may seek, generate, or compare many alternate hypotheses before reaching a conclusion. On the other hand, the motivation for closure upon a specific content, such as a verdict of "not guilty," may guide a lawyer holding a strong defense case to overlook or readily dismiss information that might contradict his specific desired verdict so as to get the judge to reach closure upon it, whereas the prosecutor may be led by a motivation for avoiding specific closure upon a "not guilty" verdict leading her to generate further alternative hypotheses.

Kruglanski has led extensive empirical research and analysis of other theories addressing motivations, satisfyingly corroborating the hypothesis that the possible permutations of his epistemic motivation matrix account for the knowledge construction and acquisition process of lay people guided by a plethora of factors. These include a variety of "motivational bases" that coalesce with his generalized epistemic motivation matrix (e.g., perceived benefits or costs of closure or nonclosure), different content domains (e.g., various belief systems), and different mental or emotional states (e.g., fatigue, alcohol, or anger) (e.g., Kruglanski 2004: 6–11).

Integration between the cognitive procedure and the matrix of epistemic motivations accompanies any regular process of knowledge construction. Every reasonable instance of knowledge construction requires that the process of hypothesis generation and validation reaches a decision point or closure, allowing the person to build upon it in order to carry on. It also requires that in the face of further or contradicting evidence closure is avoided or reversed, so that alternative hypotheses are raised and validated until there is a reasonable amount of evidence supporting one hypothesis over others. Every decision or temporary closure implies that the person has bestowed a minimal degree of confidence on the subjective knowledge underlying the chosen hypothesis, and has decided to temporarily exclude further relevant information that they could always gather on the subject. Bestowing a minimal degree of confidence, as opposed to a high degree of confidence or no confidence at all, on a hypothesis implies that the person holds it as probable, allowing its revision to accommodate new data or the raising of further alternative hypotheses in the face of contradicting data.

This orderly and reasonable search for knowledge is sometimes strongly biased by the epistemic motivations instigating and accompanying it. This occurs in situations that may generate cognitive affects that elevate an individual's epistemic motivation or need to achieve a goal. This heightening may severely constrain the orderly knowledge-acquisition process, bringing it to a hasty halt or leading to the avoidance of reaching a decision altogether, sometimes irrespective of the nature of further information (Kruglanski 2004: 11–17).

This implies that some cognitive affects disrupt the probabilistic nature of the process of knowledge construction and acquisition. Chief among the elevated epistemic motivations that Kruglanski detects are a heightened "need for closure" and a heightened "fear of invalidity." Heightened need for closure ensues when lack of closure is experienced as aversive, as when a person is time pressured to make a decision. It leads individuals to seek closure by "seizing" upon scant available data and readily available previous knowledge, and to cognitively "freeze" upon the hastily formed conclusion that affords the desired closure. Freezing implies that the concluding proposition is henceforth held with high confidence. As argued by Kruglanski and supported by empirical evidence, "[t]he higher the need for closure, the more psychologically important such [closure] gratification and the stronger the tendency to perpetuate it or lend it permanence via freezing" (Kruglanski and Webster 1996: 276). For example, research into the deliberations that preceded the Israeli government's decision to launch a preemptive strike against Egypt and Syria in June 1967 (what Israelis term "The Six Day War") has indicated that a heightened need for closure was a major factor propelling the decision. This need was elevated during what Israelis call "the waiting period," referring to the two months preceding the war during which many Israelis anxiously followed the escalating threats of war voiced by Egypt's President Nasser along with the sight of multitudes of Egyptian citizens parading in the streets and calling upon Nasser to destroy Israel. This anxiety is considered a major factor leading to the Israeli government's questionable conclusion that war was imminent and to its decision to launch a preemptive strike (e.g., Brecher 1980: 35–50, 91–170).

The other major cognitive affect having the opposite result to that of a heightened need for closure is an elevated fear of invalidity. When a person fears that reaching a wrong decision will have detrimental consequences, he/she may be propelled to seek further alternatives, often engendering a frantic search for competing hypotheses (ibid.). Kruglanski notes that need for closure and fear of invalidity do not exclude one another and invariably lead to seeking closure or generating further hypotheses. Thus, a major motivational factor engendering a heightened need for closure occurs when time pressures to make a decision are accompanied by fear of invalidity due to lack of information or a disturbing/threatening uncertainty. In such cases individuals are prone to readily accept available propositions stemming from what they consider as authoritative sources, so as to alleviate uncertainty.

Fear of invalidity may also lead individuals to fix upon nonclosure and generate "loopy thinking." Research into "learned helplessness" (e.g., Burns and Seligman 1991) indicates that under acute fear of invalidity or "evaluation anxiety" (Beck et al. 1985) individuals may fix on a mental loop whereby options are reduced to a narrow and recurring set of irresolvable alternatives, a mental maze from which they cannot escape. A good example of such "loopy thinking" can be found in the Israeli government's abstention from calling upon a full army enlistment despite obvious intelligence concerning the Egyptian and Syrian high command preparations to launch a coordinated attack on Israel in October 1973 (what Israelis call "The Day of Atonement War," where Israel suffered unprecedented casualties). Research into the deliberations of the Israeli government that preceded the war indicates what Kruglanski terms "paralysis by analysis." The abstention from enlisting the army was influenced by a fear of invalidity that engendered cyclical assessments of whether war was imminent or not, irrespective of amounting data that war was at the door. It has been suggested that this unresolved deliberation stemmed from (among other factors) the government's concern that launching another preemptive strike, now that Israel was powerful and under international critique due to its occupation of the territories it conquered during the June 1967 war, might have dire consequences for Israel in the international arena (Brecher 1980: 50–76, 170–229).

The seizing and freezing cognitive process brought about by a heightened need for closure has been shown by extensive research to have several unfavorable consequences. These include poor information processing; the inclination to accept the views of authoritative sources; salience of stereotypical judgment; high reliance on primary impressions; highly selective gathering of information that conforms to readily available mental schemes, along with disregard of information contradicting these schemes; and the inability to generate competing hypotheses to explain the situation (Kruglanski 1996: 264–269). This blocking of optional thinking by a "closed" state of mind obstructs the ability to assess or generate fruitful possible reasons, consequences, or solutions to different life problems.

Closed mindedness and the attendant lack of alternative hypothesis generation or comparison have been identified by psychologists in individual and group decision processes (e.g., Kruglanski 2004: 132–138) in deliberate self-harm patients (McAuliffe et al. 2008), in youth at risk (e.g., Benard 1991; Ungar 2001), and in groups involved in intractable conflicts (e.g., Bar Tal and Teichman 2005). This body of research focuses upon the failure of its subjects to seriously contemplate alternate ways out of their predicament. It also notices in its subjects an attendant sense of over-determination and that they lack choice, proposing various strategies for the enhancement of optional thinking as a cognitive tool that may "defreeze" closed mindedness and inculcate a sense of choice and indeterminacy (ibid.: 391–406; Kruglanski 2004: 139–145).[5]

The remainder of this book brings Kruglanski's theory of the lay epistemic process of knowledge construction and acquisition, particularly its focus upon how this process is biased by cognitive affects, to bear upon the process of film viewing. It aims to identify the ways in which films may encourage closed mindedness or loopy thinking[6] in viewers, and conversely, how they may encourage optional thinking by requiring viewers "to conceptualize options to hypothetical but typical real-life problems" (Platt and Spivack 1977: 17).

It will focus on narrative films because their comprehension requires that viewers employ a causal cognitive knowledge construction process about possible lifelike situations, experienced as very tangible given films' cinematographic and aural flow. Narrative films offer a better artifact to study how cognitive affects bias this process than the visual arts or literature which lack continuous flow and are experienced as less tangible and lifelike.

I have opted for the concept of optional thinking as defined above because, while Kruglanski's general theory of the lay epistemic process of knowledge acquisition is productive in explaining the process of alternative hypothesis generation, validation, and judgment in different domains, its application to narrative films requires that this general process concerns itself with the peculiar way in which narratives evidence or encourage in viewers a knowledge construction process. This peculiarity concerns an overall trajectory that causally chains reasons to events that engender conflicts, the conflicts to ensuing consequences, and the consequences to conflict resolutions and closures. Hence, I prefer to term the process of alternative hypothesis generation and validation in narrative films "optional thinking," since this concept as defined above is fit for analysing viewers' cognitive affective process in respect of narrative constructs.

In dealing with narrative movies, I will follow Bordwell in positing that a viewer's main cognitive motivation is to construe a story and a world out of the film's audiovisual flow (Bordwell 1985: 31). I will focus upon ways that narrative films cue or encourage cognitive affects in viewers striving to construct the film story in their minds and with how these cognitive affects encourage the biasing of the viewer's epistemic motivation to construe the story toward closed mindedness or optional thinking.

While different narrative films will be considered, particular attention is given to popular narrative films, hereby called movies. This is because movies are enjoyed by many people around the world since they allow them to carry out a process of knowledge construction that renders a clear and causally coherent narrative leading to a satisfying closure (N. Carroll 1985). They are also very influential due to the powerful cognitive affects they evoke through a relentless audiovisual flow, and the expert deployment of strategies engendering intense suspense, surprise, and empathy (Plantinga 2009; Tan 1996).

I find this research important because as I will show, the enjoyment of most movies goes hand in hand with the encouragement of closed mindedness in viewers. I do not mean to say, however, that movies encouraging closed mindedness should be univocally denounced. It is questionable whether movies encouraging closed mindedness, loopy thinking, or optional thinking meaningfully affect the different "habits of mind" viewers have.[7] Extensive empirical research is needed to establish the degree to which particular viewers' dispositions may be affected by the film-viewing process, and whether, or to what degree the watching of movies that limit optional thinking or trigger it affects viewers outside the movie theater. Movies also offer a variety of sensual, emotive, and cognitive pleasures besides the cognitive affects biasing viewers' process of knowledge construction, and there are various life experiences that may encourage optional thinking. Therefore, I do not suggest that all movies must promote viable optional thinking, but rather that this is one favorable value that a movie can have. What bothers me is that those who favor mind-closing movies are unaware of this process or think it is a necessary though negligible outcome of their popularity, wrongly presuming that encouraging optional thinking must be to the detriment of the pleasures that make movies popular. What also concerns me is that those who critique movies for reasons akin to the notion of closed mindedness share the presumption that it is a necessary correlate to what makes these movies popular and therefore "throw out the baby along with the bath water." This study shows that encouraging optional thinking in movies need not diminish what makes movies popular and enjoyable, and that encouraging optional thinking may enhance rather than reduce the cognitive pleasures afforded by movies.

1.2. The Argument

Most movies use those aspects that make them popular in a way that encourages the reduction and even blocking of the viewers' optional thinking process. Through cognitive affects stemming from the ways in which movies deploy narrative suspense, surprise, and the arousal of empathy for protagonists, narrative uncertainty is felt as distressing, thereby heightening the need to avoid it by seeking resolution and closure. This distressed expectancy for resolution focuses viewers' attention on the most salient narrative features rather than possible alternate thoughts and is then gratifyingly reciprocated by the gradual reduction of narrative optionality into a single trajectory and univocal closure, retroactively presented as strictly and necessarily ensuing from what went on before. Through this hurried and option-reducing narrative process, movies encourage the blocking of optional thinking.

This movie dynamic may imply that avoiding suspense, surprise, or a determined single closure encourages optional thinking in viewers. Indeed, there are film theories and attendant narrative films that critique movies for similar reasons. These tend to dismantle or disregard the strategies used in popular narrative films and to avoid their reductive narrative processes and univocal closure. This anti-movie approach can be found in formalist, neo-Marxist and postmodern approaches to film. I will argue, however, that these approaches imply cognitive affects that fail to encourage viable optional thinking. Formalist theories (e.g., Burch 1981; Tynianov 1981) fail because they tend to split the viewer's attention between the highlighted formal configurations and the narrative illusion; neo-Marxist theories (e.g., Althusser 1971a; Baudry 1985; Dayan 1976) fail due to the incomprehensibility resulting from their dismantling of narrative coherence and closure; whereas postmodern theory (e.g., Barthes 1977; Kristeva 1980) wrongly presumes a cognitively split viewer that can attentively follow an array of micronarratives and intertextual references, or short circuit optional thinking by devising looped narrative mazes. These theories, in their dismantling of narrative coherence and closure, cue split attention, confusion, distraction, or frustration in viewers.

Discarding these alternate theories insofar as they do not encourage optional thinking, I turn to reconsider the narrative-characteristic structure and strategies that make films popular, in an attempt to answer the question of whether these characteristics invariably encourage the blocking of optional thinking. Arguing against cognitive theories of movies that presume a highly cognitively active viewer without attending to the cognitive affects of movies, or misguidedly consider these affects as cognitively favorable, a set of suggested conditions will be offered. Movies that fulfill these may nevertheless encourage viable optional thinking through the strategies that make them popular.

Movie strategies evoking suspense, surprise, and empathy for characters result in affects that may encourage viewers to constrain their optional thinking processes if no options are suggested. However, when these strategies are reciprocated by movie narratives that compel viewers to compare and assess alternative narrative trajectories or different perspectives if they are to comprehend the coherence and narrative closure of the movie, these very same affects may strongly encourage optional thinking.

Countering claims raised by other cognitivists, I will argue that such narratives trigger cognitive activities that regular viewers can handle and that enhance their enjoyment and their gratification upon closure. This is achieved in movies that offer a coherent yet probabilistic type of narrative causality. Probabilistic causality, which is inherent in narratives to begin with, is usually masked in popular movies by their imparting an apparent sense that events in the narrative follow each other in strict and necessary causality. This sense is achieved, for example, by using the interplay of foreshadowing clues and their later recall, so important for establishing coherence precisely because narrative causality is probabilistic, in a way that lends to such clues a univocal causal meaning. However, as will be shown, later recollections of early clues can offer several optional meanings for these clues without thereby losing narrative coherence.

If a probabilistic type of narrative construct suggests optional trajectories or alternate points of view that carry enough information for viewers to construct these as viable and pertinent to the overall comprehension of the narrative, viewer suspense is enhanced by the very need to assess these viable options for comprehension. In addition, surprises, easy to implant in movies because of the viewers' heightened need for closure, need not be used to block optional thinking as is the case in most movies. The triggering of optional thinking inherent in surprise may be exploited rather than suppressed. Suspense and surprise strategies need not be reciprocated by forming a tight, linear, and single closure to be pleasurable. Movies using optional narrative tracks can offer several consecutive or parallel well structured narratives that in their converging and diverging interrelations lead to several alternative yet feasible closures *while* being suspenseful and surprising. I will elucidate this in my analysis of the popular movies *Run Lola Run* (Tom Twykers 1998) and *Sliding Doors.*

Likewise, empathy for protagonists need not be restricted to one dominant or sole protagonist and his/her outlook. Empathy can be engendered for several equally important protagonists and even for antagonists. This may enhance the viewers' optional thinking process because it leads them to take different perspectives, coordinate, and compare them. This will be shown in the analysis of Akira Kurosawa's *Rashomon* (1950), where the viewer must interlace different character perspectives for comprehension.

Finally, films do not need to provide explicit information on alternate trajectories within the movie as in the cases mentioned above. Optional thinking can also be encouraged by the evocation of well known dramatic histories or fictions as shown in the analysis of Quentin Tarantino's popular World War II counterfactual to history film *Inglourious Basterds* (2009). The movie's overlay of a counterfactual alternative upon a well known, dramatic, historical precedent can be suspenseful and evocative of optional thinking, because the predetermined trajectory and known outcome is evaluated throughout in light of the digressive alternative outlined. In fact, much of the pleasure viewers have in this film seems to concern their constant entertainment of the historical narrative, considering the ways in which the viewed version converges and diverges from it, evocatively implying that the course of history is ultimately unpredictable and different feasible outcomes may lead to alternate futures.

1.3. The Structure

This book is divided into five chapters. The first chapter or introduction (the present one) discusses the concepts of optional thinking, closed mindedness, and loopy thinking while also providing a summary of the argument made throughout the book. The second chapter considers the relation between most popular narrative films and closed mindedness from a cognitive-psychological perspective. Following a discussion of narrative, audiovisual flow, suspense, surprise, empathy for characters, and the narrative interplay of cataphora and anaphora, it argues that most movies encourage the blocking of optional thinking in viewers. This argument is instantiated through a detailed analysis of notable popular films, such as *Duel* (Steven Spielberg 1971), *Silence of the Lambs* (Jonathan Demme 1991), and *The Sixth Sense* (M. Night Shyamalan 1999). The third chapter deals in depth with the major tenets of formalist, neo-Marxist, and postmodern approaches in film studies, insofar as these approaches claim something akin to the idea that movies discourage optional thinking. It shows why such approaches, given their underlying premises, concepts, and solutions to how films may engender optional thinking offer overall failed alternatives. This will be discussed in light of movies deemed by these approaches to develop something akin to optional thinking, such as *La Chinoise* (Jean Luc Godard 1967), *Timecode* (Mike Figgis 2000), or *eXistenZ* (David Cronenberg 1999), instantiating how such films are often incomprehensible or present and may encourage a looped mental maze in a manner that impedes optional thinking. The fourth chapter reconsiders the strategies that make films popular, showing how these end up encouraging optional thinking in movies such as *Run Lola Run, Inglourious Basterds*, and *Rashomon*. The fifth chapter or conclusion of the book recapitulates the argument, suggests some underdeveloped movie strategies that may encourage optional thinking, and considers untapped strategies that may, pending further research, cue powerful optional thinking processes in viewers.

Notes

1. See also Platt et al. (1975) and Spivack et al. (1976).
2. See chapter 3 of this volume for an in-depth discussion of how the notion of "open-mindedness" informs formalist, neo-Marxist, and postmodern approaches to film.
3. This approach to problem solving has come under attack in the literature for the reasons mentioned. See, for example, Sternberg (1995: 295–321). This critique has recently led to attempts at devising problem-solving experiments that are more lifelike in their attention to the interplay of the cognitive, motivational, and social components of problem solving. Dörner, for example, utilizes very complex, computerized scenarios that contain up to two thousand highly interconnected variables (Dörner and Wearing 1995). See also Ringelband et al. (1990: 151–164) and Buchner (1995).
4. See chapter 2 for an extended analysis of Bordwell's and Tan's respective approaches.
5. Concerning optional-thinking encouragement, it seems that the "narrative therapy" approach (White and Epston 1990), based as it is on the comprehension that narrative is a fundamental way for people to make their life experiences comprehensible, may turn out to be particularly useful to encourage optional thinking. Narratives consist of arranging life experiences through dynamic schemas into a causal trajectory with a beginning, middle, and end, figuring originating events, human decisions, and their complications and consequences. Narrative therapy tries to help individuals overcome their problems by asking them to narrate their life experiences, thus "externalizing" their problems, and then offers to "re-story" these life experiences. "Re-story" implies the identification of cognitively frozen premises (e.g., stereotypes) in personal narratives, the patients' resulting reasoning of the problem, and the bringing forth of underrated experiences, memories, or other relevant people's views to help forge optional narratives that may help to solve or dissolve the problem. Hence, "re-story" implies optional-thinking training and cognitive defreezing. Narrative therapy seems to be also tightly linked to the optional-narrative movies discussed in the final chapter, in that such films audiovisually "externalize" the problems dealt with and re-story the causes and conse-

quences leading to the problem they deal with. Using narrative movies for optional-thinking enhancement using the tenets of narrative therapy may be a privileged therapeutic tool since it implies the entertainment of tangible, life-like, alternative "mental simulations." On mental simulation as a therapeutic tool see Decety and Stevens (2009: 3–20). However, the relevance of narrative therapy and mental simulation to optional-thinking encouragement and their relation to optional movies are leads that need to be developed and researched within a different framework.

6. As described above, "loopy thinking" is a term I coined to describe a mental state characterized by a subject's mental freezing upon nonclosure. This paralyzing mental state is reminiscent of the story of Buridan's Ass (attributed to Jean Buridan, a fourteenth-century French philosopher), about an ass standing at the same distance from two identical haystacks which starves to death because reason provides no grounds for choosing to eat one rather than the other.

7. Howard Margolis discusses how habits of mind may be formed, how difficult it is to change these, and what consequences different habits of mind might have. He generally defines a habit of mind as "a habitual pattern of inference or way of seeing things" (1987: 42).

2

Closed Mindedness in Movies

2.1. What Are Movies? The Current Cognitive-Psychological Approach

Cognitive approaches have offered a simple and fruitful definition of the narrative characterizing most popular narrative films. As succinctly defined by Branigan, "narrative is a way of organizing spatial and temporal data into a cause–effect chain of events with a beginning, middle and end" (1992: 2). This definition, while not inclusive of all films and certainly not of all works of literary prose,[1] is particularly apt in describing what have been called Hollywood classical film narratives as well as the many contemporary popular films that follow the latter's legacy. These films, aptly termed "movies" by Carroll, have been proven to be particularly engaging or interesting for many viewers around the world (N. Carroll 1985). Film researchers working within a cognitive psychological framework suggest that a major explanation for this widespread popularity and engagement stems from the way the narrative construction of these movies engages our cognitive faculties. They appeal particularly to our ingrained processes of knowledge acquisition which help to make the world comprehensible (Bordwell 1985: 30–40). Given the affinity between this approach and the lay cognitive process of knowledge acquisition described in the introduction, cognitive psychology seems particularly fit to discuss these movies in this study.

The cognitive psychological approach maintains that popular narrative films engage viewers because they invite them to witness and experience as satisfying a process akin to that of knowledge construction. Carroll, for example, suggests that beyond the relative ease with which we understand film sounds and images, the narrative spatial and temporal organization of audiovisual stimuli into a cause–effect chain leading to closure appeals to us, because it caters to our cognitive perceptual mode of making the world intelligible through a question–answer process. In his view, narrative films are particularly appealing because, unlike real-life situations, these movies use framing, composition, and editing to raise clear questions and provide upon closure full answers to all of the questions raised, a process that hardly gets satisfied in real life (N. Carroll 1985).

Likewise, David Bordwell has offered a comprehensive account of how viewing popular narrative films triggers our ingrained process of knowledge construction and acquisition. Maintaining that "perceiving and thinking are active, goal oriented processes" (Bordwell 1985: 31), he argues that viewers strive to construct a coherent, intelligible, goal-oriented trajectory from a film's audiovisual flow. He delineates presumed strategies and procedures that allow spectators that he considers active and aware to construct the film narrative in their minds. His presumption is that spectators strive to construct a goal-oriented story out of the film screened before them, by constantly forwarding perceptual and cognitive hypotheses (based upon schemes they have in their mind) and try to fit the film data to these. The art of filmmaking resides in the ways narrative devices guide and play with this construction process. The filmmaker presupposes this process and construes clues, surprises, distractions, diversions, and postponements that trigger hypotheses in viewers, and then verifies or refutes them. From this, claims Bordwell, derives the narrative film's appeal to spectators. Popular narrative films address the cognitive faculties of their spectators and strive to allow them to successfully build a world and a story by consciously realizing these faculties, a process they are hardly aware of, or which is hardly satisfied in real life. He further maintains that the interaction between spectator and film narrative is based upon different narrative templates viewers possess, such as the overarching narrative template of "exposition, complication, resolution." The spectator hypothesizes this template and tries to fit the film data to it. Following research by Sternberg, Bordwell delineates types of hypotheses raised by viewers in response to the narrative. These include curiosity hypotheses relating to what has happened before the film started and expectation hypotheses dealing with what will happen next. Viewers strive to verify their hypotheses as the film evolves, and tend to hold on to them or refute them according to their plausibility. Different strategies are used to verify or refute hypotheses such as a "wait and see" strategy when evidence is inconclusive. According to Bordwell, popular narrative films deeply engage and sustain the attention of viewers because they allow them in an intriguing manner to follow and construct coherent narratives leading to closure (Bordwell 1985). This is usually achieved through a systematic configuration of stylistic and plot devices rendering an overall continuous editing style, synchronized or otherwise cohering audiovisual formations, and spatial constructions arranged around the logic of the plot succession, all in a manner that offers intermittent story recentering and the leading of the plot to story closure.

Attendant to the presumed cognitive pleasures that Bordwell relates to knowledge construction, movies also strongly engage viewers emotionally. As he states, "when the narrative delays satisfying an expectation, the withholding of knowledge can arouse keener interest …. The mixture of anticipation, fulfillment, and blocked or retarded or twisted consequences can exercise great emotional power" (ibid.: 40). While Bordwell himself failed to consider in depth how movies raise emotions, other cognitivists have tackled this issue, focusing in particular upon suspense, the most salient affective structure used by movies (e.g., Plantinga 2009; Vorderer et al. 1996).

Carroll, for example, suggested a cognitive-directed emotional process to address issues of emotional concern for characters, particularly as this relates to suspense structures in movies (N. Carroll 1996b). His "thought theory of emotion" was outlined as a counter argument to the widespread notion of "suspension of disbelief" and its variants. According to the latter, the viewers' emotional involvement in fiction, particularly in fictional suspense, is derived from their belief in the reality portrayed by movies and an attendant "identification" with the camera's point of view and with characters. Given this, such theories suggest that viewers undergo the emotions that a character they identify with undergoes within a diegetic world they have somehow convinced themselves is real. Carroll argued that this position is incomprehensible. He rejected the idea of "suspension of disbelief" on the grounds that we cannot force ourselves into believing that something is true when we know it to be false (e.g., making ourselves believe that something we know is fictional is real). Likewise, he rejected the attendant notion of viewer identification with the camera or with characters as an explanation for our concern and the emotions we feel. Explaining that identification in fact means that viewers manipulate themselves or are somehow manipulated into the irrational belief that the camera lens is their own eye or that they are the protagonists, he asked: how can it be that viewers do not realize that their eye differs from that of the camera when they look aside to the person sitting near them, or walk into the theater while the movie is playing? He also asked: how can viewers find themselves in suspense when they know the protagonist is in danger, and yet the protagonist with whom they presumably identify has no knowledge of the danger he/she is in and is therefore not in suspense? (ibid.: 80, 109, 210–214). Carroll suggested instead that the viewers' comprehension of fiction and their emotional response to protagonists derive from their entertaining "what if?" propositions. He argued that "what if?" propositions that better fit a fictional world, along with thought-derived emotions of empathy or solidarity with morally favored protagonists, suffice to evoke an emotional response in viewers without their holding irrationally the belief that what is unfolding before their eyes is really happening or is really happening to them.

Carroll dealt with viewers' concern for characters particularly in respect of suspense structures. He maintained that while suspense derives from uncertainty about the outcome of a given situation, suspense also demands that we care about what it is that we are uncertain about. We might be uncertain about whether a character will button his shirt but this does not mean we are concerned about it and henceforth feel suspense. In other words, for suspense to occur, the necessary state of uncertainty needs to be about something we care about, such as a character that represents a moral standpoint we share: "The care and concern required for suspense ... are engendered for audiences of fiction by means of morality" (ibid.: 84).

While Carroll's thought-evoking-emotion theory seems plausible, as well as his empathy- or solidarity-based explanation for our concern for protagonists, his explanation of suspense as dependent exclusively upon empathy for protagonists and their values fails to account for our feeling of suspense when an antagonist is endangered. Take for example the case of the strangler in Alfred Hitchcock's *Frenzy* (1972), where we are evidently in suspense when the serial killer attempts to reach, while in danger of being caught, the incriminating pin that his last victim has torn from his lapel. Even Carroll's stretching of morality to include virtues such as beauty or courage in order to explain occasional evident suspense that concerns antagonists cannot explain away the suspense felt for Bob Rusk (Barry Foster), the ugly and fearful serial killer in *Frenzy*. Hence there must be something in movie suspense that goes beyond its mediation through moral characters we empathize with. Carroll's notion of anticipation for answers as implied in his question–answer narrative film model goes some way in this direction, but does not consider the psychological dynamics of suspense, and in particular its reciprocal effect upon the cognitive thought process itself.

These two reservations have been recently addressed by several cognitive psychologists (e.g., Grodal 2009; Plantinga 2009; G.M. Smith 2004; M. Smith 1995; Tan 1996). Ed Tan in particular, in his comprehensive book *Emotion and the Structure of Narrative Film* (1996), uses Nico Frijda's functional definition of the emotional system to address the psychological dynamics of suspense and its reciprocal effect upon the cognitive thought process. Using Fridja's functional definition of the emotion system as "geared toward establishing the relevance of certain situations for the concerns of the individual and, if such relevance exists, to enforce the priority of cognition and action in accordance with those concerns," Tan suggests that while movies respond to various concerns of viewers, such as a general concern "with the fortunes of our loved ones ... [, which] takes the form of sympathy with the fate of a particular character" (Tan 1996: 48), the most movie-specific and overarching viewer concern has to do with the reduction of "tension" (a term subsuming suspense). This tension-reduction concern relates both to the uncertainty viewers experience in the fictional world "which by the end of the film has been resolved" (ibid.: 35) and to the attendant "chaotic structural organization of the artifact, in particular its system of plot and style [that] requires a mental effort on the part of the viewer and creates a desire for order. Gradually the representation of these systems does indeed take on a more orderly form and ultimately ends in a good Gestalt" (ibid.). Hence, Tan (and others) have recently complemented the cognitive approach to popular narrative films with a consideration of emotions and of the reciprocal effects of emotional states upon cognition. Particularly important for our concern is Tan's use of Frijda's contention that the emotional system enforces "the priority of cognition in accordance with the emotional concern." Given that the major emotional concern identified by Tan as specific to movies is that of tension reduction, Tan concludes that a movie is primarily an "Emotion Machine" (the subtitle of his book) that evokes in viewers tension and the concern for its reduction. It is this concern that gears the viewers' cognitive process toward achieving tension reduction by seeking to resolve the uncertainty in the narrative world and achieve formal order. These movies, claims Tan, in a "miracle of precision" (ibid.: 251) achieved among other means by a calculated audiovisual flow that regulates the intensity of emotion (ibid.: 56–57), and by instigating in viewers a notion of their flowing along with the movie "by a well timed sequence of challenges that the viewer is just barely capable of meeting" (ibid.: 93), regulate and control the viewers' desire for tension reduction in a gratifying manner, offering along the way "the satisfaction of cognitive curiosity, the excitement, the sense of competence, [and] the enjoyment of spectacles" (ibid.: 249), resulting in a gratifying release of tension upon closure.

As this summary rendition of the comprehensive and comprehensible cognitive-psychological approach to movies suggests,[2] it seems that the challenging of the viewers' cognitive faculties in a manner that satisfyingly lets them construct out of the movies' compelling audiovisual flow a coherent story that leads to closure, along with the attendant arousal, regulation, and control of tension, mostly through suspense strategies, are the sine qua non components that account for the popularity of movies.

While cognitive approaches to film seem to have identified the major components that turn movies into popular artifacts, their lauding of the cognitive and affective pleasures afforded by movies fails to take into consideration the movies' cognitive affects and how they are deployed to encourage closed mindedness. This is the concern of our next section.

2.2. Closed Mindedness in Movies

I argue that most movies, while appealing and popular because they encourage in viewers a heightened need for closure and gratify this need in their resolution (heightened need for closure roughly corresponds to Tan's need for tension reduction as discussed above), encourage closed mindedness and the viewers' "freezing" upon the stereotypes or moral propositions presented in the movie (on "freezing" see above, 1.1. Optional Thinking and Closed Mindedness). Heightened need for closure is encouraged by the movies' proactive forward and irreversible audiovisual flow, and by the use of suspense/ surprise constructs, enhanced by the evocation of empathy for characters. Such constructs encourage a disturbing uncertainty concerning future outcomes, resulting in an enhanced need for gratifying relief through closure. While this may lead to closed mindedness, this must not necessarily be the case as will be discussed and instantiated in chapter 4. However, the way by which this proactive, elevated need for closure is reciprocated by most movies promises an effective blocking of optional thinking. As succinctly put by Polkinghorne, "Narrative exhibits an explanation instead of demonstrating it …. It explains by clarifying the significance of events that have occurred on the basis of the outcome that has followed. In this sense narrative explanation is retroactive" (1988: 21). As will be shown, in most movies, the heightened need for closure encouraged by the forward march of the movie is reciprocated by the retroactively reasoned strict reduction of options that leads to a single resolution and closure. This construing is very detailed in movies, operating both on the level of audiovisual continuity and on the level of overall plot design.

Retroactive reasoning results from narrative movies' loose probabilistic causality, which stems from the films' depiction of apparent or feasible life situations where any given outcome may be always understood as one plausible result out of several. This suggests that narrative movies, because of their ingrained loose narrative causality and audiovisual flow, can offer a powerful venue for the pleasurable development of optional thinking. Hence, through audiovisually flowing narratives, movies make events comprehensible for viewers by the arrangement of these into loose causal, audiovisual, dynamic structures with a beginning, middle, and end, figuring originating events, human decisions, and their complications and consequences. This process may gear the viewers' entertainment of offered alternatives toward their structuring into interlacing plausible, variable chains of reasons and consequences processed through evocative perceptual, cognitive, and emotional cues.

Most movies, however, rarely encourage optional thinking in their narrative structure (for such rare cases and the development of such potential see chapters 4 and 5). These films are more concerned with blocking optional thinking. While loose causality implies that at every turn of events things could move in different directions, the viewers' potential sense of freedom of choice at narrative turning points (i.e., points of potential entertainment of optional courses of action) does not usually trigger a fruitful or enjoyable consideration of options. On the contrary, as will be suggested, these movies turn the possible consideration of options into an unpleasant experience. This, as mentioned, is due to narrative movie strategies that heighten the need for a gratifying closure retroactively reciprocated by a strict reduction of options that leads to a single resolution and closure. These strategies include the arousal of the viewer's tension by means of a relentless audiovisual flow, combined with an ingrained lack of sufficient information concerning the evolving plot, not to mention the almost total lack of information concerning optional courses of action (whose potential is embedded by definition within the loose, retroactively outlined chain of causality). This process is coupled with, and enhanced by the highly unsettling uncertainty encouraged by the widespread use of strategies of suspense and surprise, along with the attendant narrowing of the viewer's perspective to that of the leading protagonist(s)—strategies that operate by withholding information. Taken together, these strategies encourage the viewer to expect and accept the retroactively reasoned strict reduction of options that lead to a single resolution and closure. This reduction is usually constructed through a play between cataphora and anaphora, whereby initial polysemous cataphors (including the more constrained cataphors known as "foreshadowing clues") are later retroactively recalled (anaphora) and made reductively and univocally significant.

I will now consider and instantiate how audiovisual narrative-film flow, suspense, surprise, and viewer-perspective focalization through protagonists, along with a particular cataphora–anaphora interplay, conspire in most movies to encourage closed mindedness in viewers.

2.2.1. Audiovisual Flow

In movies the forward-marching plot construction often proceeds through the deployment of rushing audiovisuals along the lines of what has been termed "continuity" or "analytical" editing (e.g., Bordwell 1985: 30–36). This editing system consists of assembling the various shots in such a manner that the viewer perceives them as interconnected in space and/or time, thus allowing the viewer to construe a space–time continuum. This is achieved through different strategies such as eye-line match in between shots, a bridging soundtrack, or cut on motion. In this manner the viewer is offered a relentless and irreversible plot (irrespective of whether flashbacks are used since their occurrence is always within the forward, additive, sequential plot unfolding). This cues for viewers the unsettling notion that dwelling upon vague options (based on an ingrained lack of information) may draw attention away from sudden or rushing incoming clues that are thereby perceived as important for the step-by-step and overall plot construction and comprehension.

This is in contradistinction to written texts or the visual arts, where the pace, rhythm, and overall length of experience of the work are mostly in the hands of the receivers (who can at their will invest pace, or recover any intended or immanent rhythms construed, into the work). Films, not unlike music, highly determine the viewer's experience of pace, rhythm, and length. This is certainly the case when films are projected in darkened theaters where viewers have no control whatsoever over the projection process. I think this is also the case to a large extent with television narratives, or when watching narrative films on DVD. Although in these cases the narrative flow is often interrupted by commercials or may be stopped, reviewed, or forwarded by the viewer when experienced on DVD, it seems that even such interrupted audiovisually flowing narratives are consumed in narrative chunks if they are to be somewhat experienced as intended. In other words, the willing or imposed arrest of the audiovisual flow decomposes the rhythm and pace of movies. This seems to be due to the nondiscreet nature of the phenomenology of watching movies, as opposed to reading texts or viewing visual artworks. The film flow also imparts a sense of impetus and direction which is consciously perceived when motion is arrested. Given that in audiovisual narratives this flow is directional, it commands attention to incoming and often rushing information, thereby encouraging a heightened need for repose and for closure. Coupled with this movement rush is the need to comprehend the unfolding plot, a process which requires us to try and look ahead in a manner that both aims at predicting what is coming and is open to incorporating unexpected events. In a way, this process can be compared to someone rafting down a gushing river, knowing that the waters flow in one direction (downwards, ultimately toward the sea); the faster the downward drift becomes, the more attention is required so as to successfully maintain the raft on course, and the greater the need becomes to reach the destination.[3] The cognitive effects of this audiovisual flow can be evidenced in the common "shot–reaction shot" construct. Viewers, due to the ingrained optionality in the narrative and their lay epistemic process, may implicitly expect different outcomes following a given shot. However, when the transition occurs to what has been properly termed "the reaction shot," the significance of the first shot is tightly anchored by the succeeding shot, encouraging the viewer to surrender his implicit optional thinking to the meaning engendered retroactively by the reaction shot.[4] This construct is particularly exploited in action-packed chase or dialogue sequences, where the rush of events or words, along with vague evocations of potential options, pins the viewer to the seat so as not to miss the oncoming turn of events and its attendant retroactive and restrictive meaning. This construct is also occasionally exploited for surprise effects given its apparent "automatic intelligibility" (N. Carroll 1996: 86–87). For example, a close up showing the pulling of a trigger that releases a bullet shot toward a prefigured window is expected by the viewer to smash the window in the following shot with certainty, but in the reaction shot, a flying pigeon may be surprisingly shown to intrude and deviate the bullet just before it hits the window. While such surprises may often make viewers aware of the ingrained optionality in narratives, as will be shown, this momentary awareness is exploited in such a manner that it might better pin viewers to their seats by encouraging an anxiety concerning any further incoming disruptions of expected outcomes.[5]

Except for such occasional disruptions of audiovisual flow, regular moviegoers have nevertheless frozen upon this basic level of articulation, having internalized through recurrent viewing the habitually used perceptual shot-matching schemes that render the apparent seamless continuity of these movies. Thus, when the movie complies with these habitual perceptual schemes, but for occasional disruptions that encourage the need for closure, viewers can under mild tension construct the unfolding plot in their mind while even occasionally entertaining vague optional thoughts.[6]

Popular movies, however, more often than not exploit this relatively mild audiovisual tension so as to heighten the need for closure through a combination of uncomfortably felt suspense and surprise. These strategies encourage intense attention, cueing viewers to expect and accept with gratifying relief the single resolution retroactively offered by the narrative. The next section is a consideration of how these cardinal structures operate in most movies.

2.2.2. Narrative Suspense and Surprise

The literature on suspense suggests a definition of it as an arousing yet distressful state of mind evoked by a disturbing or perceived as threatening uncertainty concerning future outcomes (Brewer 1996; N. Carroll 1996b; Plantinga 2009; Zillmann 1996). Therefore, as already discussed, suspense heightens the viewer's need for closure so as to alleviate uncertainty through a gratifying resolution (closure).[7] In general, suspense is a distressing and unsettling experience. This raises the question of why viewers are willing to experience and endure suspense in movies. In this respect I abide by Berlyne's psychobiological explanation of suspense as derived from a combination of the desire for an "arousal boost" and the desire for an "arousal jag" (Berlyne 1971; Zillmann 1996). "Arousal boost" implies that viewers desire suspense up to a point for its own sake because it makes them "feel alive," but then this desire is combined with the expectancy for an "arousal jag" implied in the satisfaction felt upon the relief from suspense. As argued by Berlyne, these two drives work in tandem to allow an organism (in this case, the viewer) to seek and reach an optimal level of satisfaction. In line with the cognitive constructivist approach guiding this study and its focus upon how thoughts trigger affective responses that in turn bias the cognitive process (particularly in fiction), I suggest that the thought-triggered heightened need for closure under suspense consists of an initial arousal boost followed by the expectancy of an arousal jag. Viewers are often willing to undergo a distressing play of suspense and relief brought about by an arousal boost engendered by a heightened need for closure, followed by the arousal jag brought about upon gratifying resolution.

As evidence suggests, a heightened need for closure reduces optional thinking, that is, the ability to generate alternative hypotheses (Mayseless and Kruglanski 1987). The reluctance to pursue new or alternative hypotheses is often due to the attendant need for further information to support these, and the possible arousal of further hypotheses. This process, under heightened need for closure, is deemed distracting and detracts from the goal to attain closure (ibid.: 269). As a follow up to this argument, I suggest that in movie suspense, where the attainment of closure is delayed and determined by the movie rather than the viewer, viewers tend to narrow the potential meanings attributed to oncoming events, objects, or characters to their valence for the advancement or retardation of closure. Moreover, under the uncertainty of suspense, viewers hold on with confidence to the movie's offered proposition as to the salient possible resolution to the suspenseful uncertainty. This often leads to their selective seizing and freezing upon information that conforms to these propositions while dismissing, twisting, or ignoring the ingrained clues that are incongruent with the confidently held movie proposition concerning the resolution of suspense.

The threat of invalidity implied in entertaining vague options that may lead to invalid and confusing plot expectations may further turn optional thinking into an unpleasant experience and condition the viewer to close down any exploration of optional explanations and readily expect and accept the authoritative signification offered by the retroactive mode of narrative reasoning (see in 1.1. Optional Thinking and Closed Mindedness, the discussion of the relation of "fear of invalidity"—when attendant to a heightened need for closure—to the acceptance of authoritative views). Rather than dwell on options that threaten comprehension, the viewer is urged to seize the option retroactively offered by the forward-flowing plot. In an apparent paradox, it is the narrative's ingrained potential for evoking optional thinking in the viewer that is used, under threat of invalid comprehension or disturbing uncertainty, to enhance the viewer's compliance with the option provided by the movie. It is the *precarious* evocation of the notion that things could turn out in different ways that reinforces the desire to seize upon the offered outcome and its retroactively reasoned meaning. This precariousness is particularly evident in surprise strategies used within suspense structures in movies.

Surprise, as defined by Meyer et al. (1992), is a reaction to a "schema discrepant event" that causes momentary cognitive confusion. Furthermore, as evidence shows, this confusion is heightened in proportion to the unexpected discrepant event's contrast with the default expected outcome (Teigen and Keren 2003). That is, the more a certain outcome is expected, the more surprising the discrepant event. Surprise, in itself, triggers optional thinking in order to try and explain the discrepancy caused by surprise. While initially this explanatory process is conducted according to readily available schemes, failure to explain through these the discrepant event may engender optional hypotheses and knowledge revisions. However, in most movies the discrepancy of surprise and the attendant potential triggering of optional thinking are deployed in a manner that encourages aversion toward optional thinking, readily blocking it while also enhancing suspense. This can be evidenced, for example, in the highly surprising scene from *The Silence of the Lambs*, where the viewer sees several shots featuring FBI agents cautiously approaching the outside of a house where they suspect the serial killer is hiding. These shots are alternated with shots of the serial killer inside a house. This triggers in the viewer the habitual parallel shot-matching scheme, combined with the inside/outside editing-transition scheme, assuring the viewer that the whole sequence occurs at the same time and in the same location: the house besieged by the FBI contains the killer. This leads the viewer to expect in suspense the result of the FBI agents' encounter with the deranged killer, and the viewer's assurance is further raised when one of the officers approaches the door and presses the doorbell, a shot strictly matched to a reaction shot of the killer seen inside his house, reacting to a doorbell ring. However, when the killer opens the door we see Clarice Sterling (Jodie Foster), the film's protagonist, whom the viewer knows to be nowhere near the house besieged by her FBI colleagues. This puzzling situation is immediately followed by a sequence showing the FBI agents storming an empty house and realizing they are at the wrong location, and by the chief agent worriedly saying "Clarice," whereby we are returned to Clarice facing the killer all alone.

The framing of surprising events within suspense structures, demonstrated masterfully in *The Silence of the Lambs* but widespread in movies, may cause the optional thinking encouraged by the surprise to be experienced adversely due to the heightened need for closure encouraged by the suspense structure. Thus, I remember that when watching the scene from *The Silence of the Lambs* discussed above, as the killer opens the door to reveal Clarice rather than the other FBI agents, I tried at first to place the FBI agents somehow at the back of the house, hoping they might come to save her. However, since the discrepancy was (too) quickly resolved by the FBI agents' realizing they are at the wrong house, I tried to think back to determine whether I should have expected this, but soon blocked that thought given the new distressing and suspenseful situation. The probable blocking of optional thoughts in such cases and perceiving them adversely results both because surprise slows down the cognitive realignment process in the face of an urgent need to keep following the new suspenseful situation (Clarice all alone), and because surprise, while valence neutral, has been shown to enhance the associated feelings of fear or anxiety that prevail in suspense structures. This turning of the potential optional thinking implied in surprise reactions into an unpleasant experience probably gears the viewer to expect and readily accept the often loose explanation for the surprising event provided by the retroactive narrative explanation (the agents too quickly realize they have broken into the wrong house and have the highly improbable clear premonition that Clarice is at that very moment far away and facing the killer alone). Once surprise is turned into an unpleasant experience, suspense and its attendant heightened need for closure are enhanced by the probable instigation of an anxiety concerning further potential unexpectedness. In many movies we may not only worry that the resolution of uncertainty ends up with detrimental consequences for our protagonist, but also fear that such a resolution will come about abruptly and unexpectedly. This is evidenced in the sequence where Clarice is descending the stairs within the killer's house in almost total darkness, encouraging us to jump in fear at any insinuation that the killer might be expecting her round a corner or will jump on her at any moment. In these cases, although we know and expect this to be possible, we fear the incumbent precise moment, which will always be unexpected (at least upon a first viewing).[8]

Another masterful example of the use of audiovisual flow and suspense/surprise structures to encourage the blocking of optional thinking can be evidenced in Spielberg's movie *Duel*. This highly suspenseful movie is totally predicated on a senseless yet relentless chase. Nonetheless, the movie occasionally leads the viewer to raise the question of why the innocent driver, David Mann (Dennis Weaver) is being hunted by a menacing truck. This occurs, for example, in an early scene where both Mann and the truck stop at a gas station. Unsure as yet of the truck driver's intention to kill him, Mann tries to get a look at him but can only see his boots. At this moment, the viewer, along with Mann, may ask themselves what the driver looks like, hoping to get a clue to his intentions. However, while this might lead the viewer to expect Mann to get out of the car and at least try a bit harder to take a look at the truck driver, Mann just takes off.[9] The evasion and deferral of this looming concern, potentially evoking optional thinking, is further blocked throughout the movie both by Mann's apparent indifference to why he is being pursued, and by his and the film's constantly reestablished proposition that the resolution of uncertainty depends solely upon how Mann will or will not manage to evade the constant attempts made by the truck driver to crush his car and kill him. In fact, Mann never considers why he is being chased even at occasional moments of repose. When, in one sequence, he manages to gain enough distance from the truck in order to hide in a side road by the highway and the truck is seen rushing past him, he dozes off. This moment of repose, however, potentially arousing different optional thoughts such as why he is being pursued, is readily interrupted by the sudden invasion of the quiet scene by an unexpected rushing train that abruptly wakes Mann and leads him on, unsuspectingly, toward the truck that awaits him down the highway, resuming from there on the suspenseful chase. In this way, suspense structures use moments of potential optional thinking not in order to cultivate that type of thinking but rather to heighten the viewer's need for closure through menacing, surprising, or unexpected events (e.g., the rushing train). Mann's need to constantly evade the truck's menace, combined with an occasional evocative yet dead-end clue to why he is being chased (e.g., by approximating yet never showing the truck driver's face), encourages the viewer to readily give up on trying to figure out why he is being chased, up until the gratifying end where the crushing of the truck and the truck driver's death make the question "why?" obsolete. The film's gratifying closure encourages both the viewer along with Mann to readily accept the movie's "jungle" morality whereby such things just happen and rather than bother with the question "why?", focus on "how" and "just do" whatever it takes to survive.

2.2.3. Perspective Taking, Empathy, and Focalization

A major component enhancing suspense and allowing the viewer's compliance with its prolongation is the viewer's empathetic relation to characters. As mentioned above, in order for viewers to feel suspense in uncertainty they need to be concerned about what is at stake. While a leading concern of viewers is their own desire for suspense and its relief as this engenders arousal boosts and jags,[10] empathy for protagonists may be a powerful way to evoke suspense by proxy, or as Zillmann puts it, protagonists provide an "empathic mediation of involvement" (Zillmann 1996: 216).

Empathy can be defined as an affective response that stems from the apprehension or comprehension of another's emotional state. This emotional concern has been shown to stem from the top-down cognitive process of taking the perspective of others, that is, the ability to see and consider things from a point of view other than one's own (Galinsky and Ku 2004; Galinsky and Moskowitz 2000; Mead 1934; Oswald 1996). A study conducted by Lamm, Batson, and Decety (2007) showed that humans' responses to the pain of others can be modulated by asking participants, who were watching a video of a medical patient in pain, to cognitively adopt and imagine the perspective of that person, or of themselves in that person's situation; or to view the patient in a detached manner. The combined results of behavioral measures and of functional magnetic resonance imaging clearly indicated that the cognitive appraisal in both the "imagine other" and "imagine self" situations engendered empathy for the patient in participants, as opposed to the detached appraisal situation. However, the intensity of empathic emotion was higher in the "imagine other" appraisal than in the "imagine self" appraisal because in the latter case empathy for the other was combined with a strong sense of aversion.

The concept of perspective taking and the attendant empathy for others goes a long way in explaining viewers' relationship to movie characters. It offers an explanation for how we can feel emotions toward fictional characters by entertaining "what if?" thoughts rather than resorting to irrational beliefs in the reality of the fictional world or identification with fictional characters. Furthermore, contrary to the notion of identification with characters, taking a character's perspective (which implies by definition that we take it to be other than our own) explains how we easily and empathically adjust to character twists or to their noncompliance with our expectations.

Carroll may be right in suggesting that empathy for protagonists results from our sharing their morality. This, however, is not the exclusive or even primary motivation for empathy. For example, we empathize with Marion (Janet Leigh) in Alfred Hitchcock's *Psycho* (1960) and are in suspense when she immorally steals from her boss, well before she becomes the prospective victim of Norman Bates (Anthony Perkins). In a way, we also feel empathy toward Bates when we are given information about the grounds for his mental disturbance, allowing us to cognitively entertain the perspective of this deranged, immoral killer. Thus, while morality may be ground for empathy, I suggest that in order to feel empathy for a character it is more important to have knowledge, particularly intimate knowledge about him/her. The cognitive perspective-taking process that encourages empathy proceeds according to our usual process of knowledge construction in general focused in this respect on our learning about others by trying to understand their point of view (Krauss and Fussell 1991). The more we know about a character, the more we come to understand the thoughts, motives, and emotions they have concerning the different situations in which we witness them in. This process familiarizes us with them and we feel empathy toward them.

Evoking empathy for characters may be used to encourage optional viewer estimates. This can happen in situations when a character acts against the viewer's good judgment and is proven right, or when the character complies with the viewer's expectation but finds deeper trouble than the viewer had hoped for or expected. This process may engender optional thinking once the inbuilt divide between protagonist and viewer is exploited to enhance a complex engagement. As will be discussed in chapter 4, perspective taking and the attendant empathy for characters may be aroused toward different characters, including antagonists, thus offering a powerful source for cueing optional thinking in viewers once they are urged to correlate and assess different character perspectives.

While cognitive perspective-taking appraisals evoke empathy, once empathy is triggered it may nevertheless bias the process of perspective taking favorably toward viewing situations and other people from the presumed point of view and evaluation of the person or character toward whom we feel empathy (Krauss and Fussell 1991). This may prevent or bias our consideration of the perspectives of people or characters about which we have less knowledge or less intimate knowledge. This empathy-engendered, unifocal perspective taking predisposes us to lean toward the views and morals of those we are empathetic toward rather than those we know less about.

Popular narrative films in particular are powerful frameworks for evoking perspective taking in viewers and may thereby engender empathy for protagonists. This is mostly due to such movies' elaborate system of narration through point of view deployment, extensively analysed in Bordwell's discussion of the varying authorial sources of narration (Bordwell 1985: 57–61), in Murray Smith's detecting of strategies of "alignment" and "allegiance" (Smith 1995), and in Branigan's levels of "focalization" (Branigan 1992: 100–107). Of particular relevance in this respect is Branigan's notion of character "focalization" through "external" and "internal" points of view. External point-of-view shots represent the character's awareness and experiences from the outside. This is particularly engaging when close ups of the character are used, since, as widely discussed by Balazs (1970), close ups engender a sense of intimate knowledge of the character's emotional situation. Such external shots are complemented by internal "focalization" shots representing a protagonist's "subjective" point of view and experience of the narrative events, by showing events, dreams, or memories as if seen through the protagonist's own eyes or from within his/her mind. This use of point of view offers viewers information on the evolving narrative from the perspective of a protagonist within the fiction. Through this process of narration the viewer in fact takes the perspective of the character on the situations presented, a process conducive to the viewer's empathic concern for the character.

However, while perspective taking can offer ways to evoke optional thinking in viewers, most movies focus the narrative through a single protagonist, thereby biasing and narrowing the viewer's experience of the narrative and of other characters to that of the leading protagonist. This process is further narrowed when the protagonist is positioned within threatening, disturbing, or embarrassing (mostly in comedies)[11] situations, encouraging both the viewers' empathy and their state of suspense.

This suspenseful mediation of the viewer's involvement through enhanced empathy for a protagonist's well being doubly encourages a heightened need for closure. This may lead viewers to narrow and reduce their attention to occurrences, ideas, compositional concerns, and other characters, particularly antagonists, exclusively, as Carroll puts it, in terms of their valence for the protagonists' success or defeat (N. Carroll 1996b).

The conflation of suspense and empathy corresponds, in terms of heightened need for closure, to such closure being dependent upon both the viewer's drive to reach a *specific* resolution (resulting in *this* character's well being) and the desire to reach *any* resolution so as to relieve the uncertainty of the suspenseful situation.[12] This conflation is what both encourages the viewer's compliance with the movie-determined prolongation of suspense (particularly when the odds against the liked protagonist are larger than those in his favor) and the viewer's sense of gratifying relief upon closure even if the liked protagonist ends up dead, as in *A Million Dollar Baby* (Clint Eastwood 2004) or *The Sixth Sense*.

In movies, the conflation of empathy and suspense, in their double encouragement of the viewer's need for closure, are conducive to the viewer's seizing and freezing upon the resolution suggested by the movie while blocking optional thoughts which are perceived as aversive.

2.2.4. The Interplay between Cataphora and Anaphora

A major narrative strategy used to enhance the viewer's seizing and freezing upon the authoritative options suggested by a movie concerns a specific play between cataphora (early cues) and anaphora (the later recall of these clues). In and of itself the interplay of cataphora and anaphora is a major strategy for construing the sense of coherence in narratives.[13] Cataphora, or the less polysemous associated idea of "foreshadowing," are tropes that outline the horizon of optional developments within the narrative, while anaphora operates by retroactively actualizing for viewers a given trope as cataphora or foreshadowing, thereby suggesting its pertinent signification for the evolving narrative trajectory. This interplay imparts a sense that what occurs within the narrative is not mere happenstance or arbitrary and that the chain of events has an internal logic that proceeds along a probable causality whereby the grounds for advanced events derives optionally from what previous events have established. It should be noted that in principle, although generic

conventions may predispose viewers to perceive certain early clues
as foreshadows or cataphora, as implied in Chekhov's famous dictum that "If in Act I you have a pistol hanging on the wall, then
it must fire in the last act" (Rayfield 1997: 203), *all* early narrative
material may be actualized retroactively as cataphora. Thus beyond
anaphoric reactivation of conventions (e.g., an early childhood discrepant incident will be functional later, an early stated prohibition
is anaphorically transgressed), anaphora can retroactively actualize
something as cataphora without any meaningful previous under-
lining: In Steven Spielberg's Jaws the inadvertent mention of an
explosive tank on the boat at the beginning of the movie becomes
anaphorically significant toward the end since this tank kills the
shark (Wulff 1996: 6). In a way, the simple insertion of new information pertaining to the past may also forge that sense of coherence (e.g., through a flashback to an as yet unseen past event
or through new evidence about the past such as a photograph).
Such anaphoric actualization may be explicit (e.g., by flashbacks
or dialogue) or implicit, whereby a certain conclusion cannot be
understood without the viewer's recall of its retroactively reasoned
cataphora trajectory. This cataphora–anaphora interplay is a major
strategy used to construct the macrolevel retroactive reasoning in a
narrative, complementing the microlevel retroactive reasoning embedded in the evolving, moment-to-moment shot chaining (see in
section 2.2.1. Audiovisual Flow, for discussion of the "shot–reaction
shot" construct).

Chekhov's dictum, however, was intended or has been interpreted
by a widespread narrative tradition to go beyond the mere instantia-
tion of such cataphora–anaphora interplay, to indicate that nothing
in a narrative should be left *univocally* unreasoned. Thus, if you put
a gun in the first act and it is not clearly and univocally retroactively
reasoned then you have constructed a poor narrative. This demand,
however, is not only simply unnecessary in terms of coherence, but
is actually unfeasible given any narrative's sound/image meaning
overflow and ingrained loose causality. Such demand simply means
imposing an apparent and ultimately unreasoned sense of strict and
exclusive causality, along with encouraging the closed mindedness at-

tendant to deterministic or fatalistic viewpoints.[14] Most movies abide by this narrative tradition by usually imparting an apparent notion of strict causality upon resolution. A major factor supporting this in terms of narrative structure has to do with an overlay of a macrostructure, consisting of univocal cataphora–anaphora retroactive reasoning, over a microstructure consisting of the shot-by-shot, strict, retroactive reasoning weaving the plot. Thus, while the microstructure outlines a trajectory that encourages viewers to block their entertainment of the ingrained optionality of the story through the way that audiovisual flow, surprise, suspense, and character empathy are deployed, the macrolevel cataphora–anaphora interplay short circuits possible accumulated optional digressions by anaphorically referring viewers further back in the story to already figured (or added) material, construing it as a strict causal chain of cataphoric antecedents. In this manner, most movies use the cataphora–anaphora interplay not merely to establish a needed coherence, but also to further strictly narrow down and block ingrained options so as to impart an apparent sense that the chain of events was predetermined; that there was no way things could have taken a different course than the one proposed, which is retroactively and univocally reasoned by the movie and resolved in a single, reductive resolution and closure.

The viewers' encouragement to expect the movie's incoming propositions explains the ease with which moviegoers often disregard, dismiss, forget, and twist even salient cataphora or foreshadowing clues that diverge from them. In most movies these inadvertent and often misleading clues, opening vague, dismissed, or twisted options upon their first appearance in the movie, if later anaphorically recalled as having a univocal meaning, support the strict narrowing down and blocking of options (see the following discussion of anaphoric recouching in *The Sixth Sense*).

This strategy, however, also allows for narrative twists and powerful surprises once early vague or inadvertent cataphora and foreshadowing clues are retroactively and explicitly anaphorically recalled, and causally recouched within a different option. As will be discussed in chapter 4, this recouching may be functional for evoking viable optional thinking. However, most movies, when using such a strategy, particularly toward the end of popular mystery films, present the new option within a surprise/suspense structure that elevates the viewers' need for closure. They offer this new option as a quick conclusion, strictly retroactively reasoned in a flash (usually a flash of recognition for both viewer and protagonist), thus encouraging a blocking of viewers' attempts to entertain this new option in respect of the previous one. In this sense, such movies, while actualizing the narrative's ingrained optionality, block its viable entertainment by obliterating and excluding the previously proposed proposition, exchanging it in a flash with the new one which henceforth becomes the sole, exclusive, and single resolution to the movie.

This process is masterfully deployed in *The Sixth Sense*. In this movie, the viewer, along with the protagonist, a child psychologist named Dr Malcolm Crowe (Bruce Willis), surprisingly realize toward the end that what they thought were the delusions of a young boy named Cole Sear (Haley Joel Osment), who claimed to be able to talk to "dead people," were real—within the fiction. Then, another powerful surprise ensues at the very end when Dr Crowe and the viewers realize that Dr Crowe, who was seen to be shot at the beginning of the movie but has apparently recovered, was in fact one of those dead people and had been dead from the very beginning without realizing this.

The first twist, whereby the viewer along with Crowe are led to realize ghosts exist, is highly surprising. However, the viewers' surprise is not due to the ghost option being suddenly made feasible. In fact, this option is intimated throughout the movie through the boy's mother's (Lynn Sear) sudden detection of a shining in all of the boy's photographs, through a scene where the mother reenters the kitchen and suddenly all the drawers open without the boy having time to do it himself, through the tangible, scary, and horrifying images of the ghosts, and through the boy's insistence that they exist. Most viewers are nevertheless surprised because they had been led up to this point to forego as optional the movie's intimation that ghosts exist, encouraged to take Crowe's perspective upon the events through Crowe's voice over and his predominant point of view. What turns this twist of events into such a surprise is the empathy engendered in viewers by their taking Crowe's perspective as dominant, thereby giving them intimate knowledge of how he perceives events (we follow his painful, misguided perception of his wife's drifting away from him toward a new young lover, we evidence his dedication to help the maladjusted boy), along with the deployment of his perception within a highly suspenseful trajectory that mainly concerns his attempt to help the scared boy and rid him from what Crowe perceives as Cole's terrible delusional visions. Thus, even though viewers also see the boy's perspective and empathize with him, this empathy is biased and mediated by Crowe's dominant perspective so that we empathize with what we perceive through Crowe as the boy's delusions, rather than with the reality of his visions. This empathy and suspense heighten the viewers' need for a relieving closure, leading us to selectively "seize" upon information that fits Crowe's perspective, disregard evidence that contradicts it, and thereby block the viability of the intimated option that ghosts exist. Viewers are also highly surprised when the twist is offered, due to the audiovisual escalation of suspense within which the revelation that ghosts exist occurs. This revelation, while being faint in terms of what supports it—Crowe plays an old recording back and forth to discern a murmur he attributes to ghosts—is suspenseful because of the tense music and recurring, escalating close ups of Crowe's face, disturbingly reacting to the murmurs he slowly discerns, intercut with escalating close ups of his finger playing with the rewind and forward buttons of the tape recorder, and ending with an extreme close up of his finger raising the volume level. The "revelation," construed through an audiovisual suspense structure taken from Crowe's perspective, encourages viewers to immediately accept and "freeze" with relief upon this twist, rejecting in a flash the option withheld up to that point that ghosts do not exist.

Upon this initial surprise, whereby Crowe realizes that ghosts exist, a gratifying resolution ensues when the boy, with Crowe's help, overcomes his fear of the ghosts he sees and starts helping them to finally rest in peace by fulfilling their last troubling wish (e.g., the boy, with Crowe as witness, helps a girl ghost that has been poisoned by her mother to reveal the deed to her grieving father).

However, even at this point most viewers do not consider as viable the option that Crowe himself is a ghost, despite the fact that this option has already been clearly hinted at when the boy intimated to Crowe early on that he sees dead people and can talk to them. Moreover, after the viewer realizes that within the fiction ghosts remain ghosts as long as they have something unresolved, the viewer still does not understand that Crowe is a ghost when the boy suggests that Crowe resolves the question of whether his wife loves him by talking to her *in her sleep*. This is also because the viewer clings in empathy and suspense to Crowe's perspective, "seizes" information conforming to it, and then freezes with relief upon the surprising "revelation" that Crowe is a ghost. This surprise encourages the viewers to freeze upon the "fact" that Crowe is a ghost because it is also placed within a suspense structure—while Crowe talks to his sleeping wife (Olivia Williams) and she responds, suddenly Crowe's wedding ring drops from her hand to the floor, swirling in close up, followed by a shot where Crowe notices his hand lacks the ring and realizes he is dead.

In this second surprise, most viewers are shaken upon realizing along with Crowe that he has been a ghost from the very beginning of the movie. This may be due to the preceding relief brought about by the resolution of the first surprise (ghosts exist) and the fear of further unpleasant surprises in the sense of "once bitten twice shy." It may be that because of this instilled fear of further surprises, viewers, upon being surprised again within a renewed audiovisual suspense construct, accept with gratifying relief the final movie resolution and closure, despite the fact that it leaves their beloved protagonist dead. That is, the need for the *specific* closure that Crowe overcomes his troubles is overcome by the need for *any* closure so as to relieve tension.

These subsequent surprises (first that there are ghosts, and second that Crowe is a ghost), due to the movie's suspense structure and the viewer's attendant heightened need for closure, exclude in a flash the viable option sustained by the movie up to each surprise (first, that there are no ghosts, and second, that Crowe is not a ghost). This exclusion occurs despite the fact that each option could have been upheld by viewers across the surprises by, for example, their raising the hypothesis that Crowe himself has become delusional (to even include within this hypothesis the whole scene of the boy's presenting the grieving father with the evidence of his daughter's murder given him by the girl ghost). What eventually ensures the viewers' exclusion of previously held options is the use of the cataphora–anaphora interplay that encourages the apparent notion that only the surprising option is each time exclusively true to the fiction to begin with. Hence, at the end, upon Crowe and most viewers realizing in agony that Crowe is a ghost, brief, quickly edited flashbacks are given that anaphorically recouch in a univocal way the cataphoric shots as apparently being exclusively compatible with the new proposed option. This, for example, is why viewers are willing to exchange "in a flash" their previous, rationally held proposition that Crowe was shown sitting sad and silent in front of his equally silent and sad wife because of their deteriorating marriage.[15] Viewers are now willing to anaphorically recouch this scene exclusively to indicate that his wife was silent simply because she was grieving and could not see him, given he was a ghost. They thereby accept with relief, imparted also upon the character, the resolution whereby their beloved character is dead as exclusive, even despite the fact that this involves an agonizing realization on their and the character's part.[16]

This strategy is also evident in Roman Polanski's movie *The Ghost Writer* (2010). It tells the story of a writer (Ewan McGregor) contracted to rewrite the memoirs of a former British prime minister named Adam Marshal (Pierce Brosnan) after Marshal's previous ghost writer was found dead. As the movie progresses we are gradually led along with the writer to discover secret photographs from Marshal's youth (a retroactively added cataphora). In these photographs, Marshal is seen with a Yale professor (Tom Wilkinson) who, as it turns out, was a CIA agent, thereby implying that Marshal may be himself a CIA agent. This proposition is also explicitly voiced by the former secretary of state and Marshal's nemesis (Robert Pugh) after Marshal has fired him. It is further grounded upon the writer secretly stealing and reading his predecessor's manuscript of Marshal's memoirs, in light of a hint left by the latter concerning "the beginnings" in his manuscript. Reading Marshal's "beginnings" leads the ghost writer to further conclude that Marshal is a CIA agent. The movie proceeds toward establishing this proposition as exclusive due to an escalating suspense trajectory enhanced by our writer being followed by CIA agents that want to murder him, and through offering vague and undeveloped hints of other possible suspects, such as a Chinese maid who looks suspiciously at him, or Marshal's secretary (Kim Cattrall), who is strongly envied by Marshal's wife Ruth (Olivia Williams). This latter proposition is somewhat enhanced when Ruth, upon learning from the writer of his suspicion that his predecessor might have been murdered, seduces him into making love to her, leading the viewer to attribute this to her pity for the worried author, her jealousy toward Marshal's secretary and her loneliness. Toward the end of the movie a rush of events ensues, beginning with the writer confronting Marshal with his suspicion and getting an angry yet not absolving reply, followed by Marshal's sudden murder by a grieving father who blames Marshal throughout the movie for his son's death in the Iraq War. This rather contrived murder,[17] resolving the suspense and apparently confirming the sole developed proposition presented, whereby Marshal was a CIA agent, is followed by a scene showing the launch of our ghost writer's posthumous "autobiography" of Marshal. This event is also attended by Ruth, the Yale professor, and our writer. At this point, the ghost writer, having been reminded of his predecessor's "the beginnings" hint, suddenly rushes to the latter's manuscript to slowly learn that "the beginnings" referred to paragraph beginnings in the manuscript rather than to Marshal's told beginnings. The writer's hurried and suspenseful arrangement of the beginning words in consecutive paragraphs[18] ends up forming a sentence which states that Ruth is a CIA agent. This leads the viewer to anaphorically recall in a flash previous scenes figuring Ruth, which s/he now tries to recall as strictly conforming to the new and surprising proposition. However, this surprised engendered memory recall, not shown in the movie and difficult for the viewer to memorize, is biased toward being exclusive because it is evoked within a suspenseful structure. Hence, upon reading that Ruth is a CIA agent the ghost writer lets Ruth know what he thinks she is, at which she immediately becomes angry toward him, an approach arrested by the Yale professor, who is seen calming her down. This is immediately followed by the writer's hurried exit toward the street where a car that is suddenly seen speeding toward him runs him over and kills him. In this movie (as in *The Sixth Sense*) the viewer is led to expect and accept this surprising new option as exclusive, despite the fact that this need not be the case, particularly since the movie does not explain how the car driver that ran him over immediately as he stepped out onto the street could have known he revealed Ruth's secret or that he would hurriedly step out right into the middle of the street. For example, the viewer could easily maintain across the surprise the very feasible option he was led to hold as exclusive up until the surprise, whereby Ruth being a CIA agent does not preclude Marshal from being one. However, I doubt this to be the case with most viewers.

The analysis of these two mystery films reveals how optionality is inherent in any narrative. The movies could have ended before the twist without offering an incoherent narrative trajectory. Their surprising optional twist testifies to the ease with which any narrative can develop as viable and coherent more than one optional trajectory, which in these two movies is simply blocked up until the surprising twist.[19] This is emblematic of how most movies manage to block the viewer's entertainment of possible options inhering in the probable causality of narratives. They do this by construing a suspense structure enhanced by an attendant evoked empathy for the leading protagonist and his perspective; by not providing enough information for the viewer to consider the necessarily but vague aroused options as feasible; and by reciprocating the viewer's suspense/empathy-enhanced need for closure in forging an apparent sense of strict causality through the interplay of cataphors and anaphors that complements the apparently strict causality retroactively imposed by the relentless audiovisual flow. These movies also evidence how movies may block the optional-thinking process that surprising events might engender in viewers. By figuring these surprises within suspense structures that encourage the viewers to experience the surprise aversively, viewers are encouraged to expect and readily accept the surprising, offered resolution as the exclusive option that is true to the fiction. Through these strategies, most movies effectively encourage closed mindedness and the blocking of the optional-thinking process in viewers. The evocation by most movies of a heightened need for closure and its implications for optional thinking undermine a leading premise underlying the cognitive-psychological approach to film delineated above, concerning the cognitively active, questioning, or hypothesizing movie viewer. While, as mentioned, the cognitive-psychological approach is the most akin to the cognitive-constructivist process of knowledge construction guiding this study, and while it has offered the most plausible explanation and description of the narrative structure of most of these films, it has so far either failed to seriously consider cognitive affects (e.g., Bordwell, Carroll) or has lauded the pleasures afforded by such cognitive affects irrespective of their encouraging the blocking of optional thinking and attendant closed mindedness (e.g., Tan).

Notes

1. There are types of films and literary works with narrative trajectories as described above that are hard or even impossible to trace, as is the case for example with films and books organized according to an association based "stream of consciousness" logic rather than upon the narrative principles outlined (e.g., Alain Resnais's 1961 film *Last Year at Marienbad* or James Joyce's 1922 novel *Ulysses*). Narratologists have contested most components of this definition, particularly the idea that a beginning-middle-end structure is a necessary component of narratives, or even the notion that narratives must relate events causally (e.g., Richardson 1997). Some have suggested that what is of the essence of narrative is change rather than causal change, or that causal change need not lead to closure for a work to be considered a narrative work. I suspect however, that while there are many such films and literary works, they present faulty or partial narratives. That is, they include narrative components but do not develop these into full-blown narratives. I contend that change without causality or causality that does not lead to an end are comprehended by readers or viewers within the context and expectation for causal trajectories leading to an end. The fact that many works often deliberately disjoint this narrative tendency may have various effects upon viewers or readers, but these effects

cannot be thought of without the context and expectations of what narratives are. The popular narrative films discussed throughout this book are characterized by their presenting a distilled and full-blown deployment of the basic and necessary components of narrative.

2. This approach seems superior in respect of viewer comprehension and affect to competing explanations. Structural approaches to popular narrative films (e.g., Schatz 2003: 92–103) discuss the definition and structure of narratives with very rudimentary and generalized tools to address the cognitive and affective process undergone by readers or viewers as they construct the narrative in their minds, a position originating in Claude Lévi-Strauss's synchronic analysis of myths (1963) and in Vladimir Propp's structuration of diachrony (1968). Psychoanalytic approaches on the other hand, whether Freudian or Lacanian (e.g., Metz 1986), base their analyses upon complex "unconscious" and unverifiable theoretical constructs (e.g., the Freudian "Oedipal complex" or the Lacanian "mirror stage") that allow for different and contradicting interpretations that prevent any prospect of orderly empirical evidence gathering rather than detailed and empirically verifiable cognitive and affective processes (for an elaborate recent critique of psychoanalytic approaches to film see Plantinga 2009: 18–47).

3. This metaphor recalls Peter Grodal's (2009) PECMA flow model of spectatorship. However, while Grodal's model may fruitfully account for bottom-up and automatic viewer responses, his prioritizing of the neuropsychological and evolutionary psychological substratum as determining film cognition overall fails to pay due attention to the overall determining function of conscious top-down cognitive processes, particularly in respect of nonsurvival situations such as watching movies.

4. This argument might recall Althusser on the functioning of ideology, in that the "subject's illusion" of freedom is exploited in order to instill ruling ideologies (Althusser 1971a: 127–188), as well as Daniel Dayan's implementation of this Althusserian argument in his analysis of the shot–reaction shot construct (1976). The reasoning for my argument largely differs from theirs as does the resulting solution since, as will be explained later, Althusser's and Dayan's conception is flawed and their resulting deconstructive resolutions offer failed alternatives (see section 3.2. The Neo-Marxist Approach: Narrative Deconstruction).

5. These fast-paced visual shifts have been aggressively exploited by the Soviet avant-garde film movement, particularly by Sergei Eisenstein in his conflict-based montage sequences (Eisenstein 1949). See, in particular, Eisenstein's editing of the "Odessa Steps" sequence in *Battleship Potemkin* (Sergei Eisenstein 1925).

6. This habitual mastering of rushing audiovisuals and its "making room" for thinking of other matters can be evidenced in car drivers. It was also noticed by Walter Benjamin in his discussion of film-viewer responses to audiovisual "shocks" (1969).

7. As mentioned, a major cause for a heightened need for closure concerns time pressures to reach a decision on inconclusive evidence. This explains for example

the intense suspense aroused by the widespread use of "last-minute rescue" constructs, a movie structure invention attributed to D. W. Griffith and used in *The Battle of Elderbush Gulch* (1913) where a group of white people is being attacked by a multitude of Indians while the cavalry rushes to the scene, arriving to the viewers' relief at the last minute. It also explains the extensive use of countdowns with potential detrimental consequences as in *High Noon* (Fred Zinnemann 1952); the use of ticking bombs threatening to blow up the protagonists, as in the James Bond movie *Goldeneye* (Martin Campbell 1995); or the extensive use of deadlines for important events that have to be met on time (meetings, weddings, the neglected child's school play, etc.).

8. It is probably the case that suspenseful, anxious expectation of surprise recurs also upon second viewing. In this I tend to agree with Carroll who claims that film recidivists experience suspense because while they may remember how suspense is resolved (as well as when a surprise is incumbent), their empathy for the endangered protagonist gears them towards sharing the protagonist's ignorance of the incumbent attack and their suspense stems from this consideration of the protagonist's state of mind (N. Carroll 1996b: 71–93). We feel suspense with Clarice when she descends the stairs because we take her perspective on the situation and imagine what she is going through. See a discussion of empathy and character-perspective taking in the upcoming section.

9. This plausible yet loosely reasoned optional action of Mann (he is afraid to look or he must hurry) results in the retroactive reduction of the semantic signification of the truck driver's boots to their being menacing, a signification reinforced as the movie proceeds and implanting the stereotype about truck drivers and trucks as senseless, potentially menacing road killers. See further elaboration of the gradual reduction/restriction of potential meanings in popular movies in the section on the cataphora–anaphora interplay.

10. This is why people probably ride rollercoasters or feel suspense when "perceptually attacked" by swirling, accelerating, or contrasting film shots figuring tornadoes, snow avalanches, or car chases.

11. Movie comedies are a special case, exhibiting peculiar strategies for evoking suspense and surprise. Their discussion merits a separate study.

12. On the need for specific closure as differing from the need for any closure, see Kruglanski (2004: 4–17).

13. Another strategy for construing coherence on the macro level of the narrative can be deduced from Bordwell's discussion of primacy. Recalling the beginning of a movie upon its ending may forge such coherence, due to the primacy effect (Bordwell 1985: 38).

14. In this sense, Chekhov's dictum belongs to a long narrative tradition that can be traced back to Sophocles' *Oedipus Rex*, one of its most prominent examples. In this play, Oedipus tries to evade his foreshadowed fate as made known to him by the Delphi Oracle, only to tragically realize through the final anaphora, that in his attempt to evade his fate he did murder his own father and marry his mother as predicted by the Oracle. Oedipus's self-blinding at the end of the play can be taken to symbolize his self-effacement at not being able to realize that his own

deeds, aimed at diverting his predetermined fate, brought him to meet his destiny. This interpretation of his self- blinding, however, is not reasoned within the tragedy's narrative trajectory, since Oedipus had no way of knowing that he was adopted and therefore could not "see" what was coming when he fled his adoptive parents' house to avoid the prophecy.

In fact, Oedipus's blinding himself has more to do with the futility of his attempt to evade his destiny than with a deserved punishment for not having seen something that could be avoided. The paradox resides of course in the play's implication that Oedipus "chose" to evade his destiny but it in fact implies, for its resolution, that there is no free choice: Not only was Oedipus destined to kill his father and marry his mother, but he was also destined to try and evade this fate, to encounter his fate, to realize this, and to blind himself. Ultimately, *Oedipus Rex* is about the lack of free choice. However, the lesson imparted by the play is achieved by construing an apparent sense that Oedipus's deeds, undertaken out of his apparently free choice, led by necessity to fulfillment of the prophecy. This is apparent rather than actual since there is nothing but happenstance and coincidence to explain how he came to murder his father and marry his mother. Neither the fact that Oedipus fled his adoptive parents, because he feared that if he stayed he would kill his father and marry his mother, nor every consequent twist in the narrative leads us to necessarily imply, even in retrospect, that he should have met his real parents. In other words, the particular narrative trajectory of *Oedipus Rex* is incidental to its conclusion. Under the prophecy, Sophocles could have written an unlimited number of narratives that could end in the same manner.

15. For how viewers were led to rationally uphold the first option in this and the other flashback scenes at the end, see Barratt (2009: 62–86). It should be pointed out that viewers could not have accepted the surprising option if it was not viable throughout the movie, including within the scenes analysed by Barratt. Hence, when these scenes are viewed for the first time, there is a vague sense of their being tentative, a sense that extends to various other portions of the film. I, for example, felt a vague unease when the movie jumped from Crowe being shot to him seated apparently well and alive at a park bench, as well as when he sat silently in front of his wife or besides the boy's mother. I remember attributing this at the time to bad directorial work.

16. *The Sixth Sense* brilliantly reflects in Crowe the cognitive process undergone by the viewers, in that Crowe's cognitively biased comprehension of what is occurring is similar to the cognitively biased way in which the viewers are encouraged to view it.

17. The script is full of loopholes and blunt contrivances, such as when the ghost writer is suddenly allowed to leave Marshal's house with the up-till-then highly guarded manuscript of his deceased predecessor. The most salient loophole is at the end when the writer is apparently purposely run over by a speeding car whose driver has no way of knowing he would step out into the middle of the street. I will further discuss this ending below.

18. This is reminiscent of a similar suspenseful strategy used by Polanski in *Rosemary's Baby* (1968) where Rosemary (Mia Farrow), following a hint as to one

of Satan's nicknames in a book given her by a friend that died in mysterious circumstances, slowly discovers by playing around with Scrabble letters, that the nickname is an anagram of her neighbor's name. This chilling realization obliterates in a flash the still somewhat viable proposition that she might be delusional (but which could be still held to be viable even after this revelation and her ensuing encounter with her baby, briefly seen through her eyes as a little devil).

19. This type of suspenseful overturn toward the end can be evidenced in several recent movies, such as *The Others* (Alejandro Amenabar 2001), *The Usual Suspects* (Bryan Singer 1995), or *Shutter Island* (Martin Scorcese 2010). Other, older movies include *No Way Out* (Roger Donaldson 1987), *Planet of the Apes* (Franklin J. Schaffner 1968), and *The Cabinet of Dr Caligari* (Robert Wiene 1920).

3

Failed Alternatives to Optional Thinking

The movie dynamic analysed in the previous chapter and its usual result of closed mindedness may imply that avoiding suspense, surprise, or a determined single closure may release viewers from the movie's grip and encourage optional thinking. Indeed, there are film theories and attendant narrative films that imply a critique of popular movies for similar reasons. These theories tend to dismantle or disregard the strategies used in popular narrative films and to avoid the films' reductive narrative processes and univocal closure. This antimovie approach can be found in formalist, neo-Marxist, and postmodern approaches to film. These three major film theory paradigms may be construed as claiming something akin to the idea that movies unfavorably encourage closed mindedness. In this chapter I discuss the nature of their critique of movies and the value of their suggested film alternatives for encouraging optional thinking.

3.1. The Formalist Approach: Form over Narrative

Following a presentation of formalist tenets and of how such tenets have influenced different film scholars, this section considers how the formalist approach may be taken to imply optional thinking strategies, concluding in the assertion that formalism, overall, offers a failed alternative to the encouragement of optional thinking.

3.1.1. Formalist Tenets

Formalism in art is based on the premise that art's uniqueness consists of abstracting and "defamiliarizing" different aspects of daily life, so as to break standardized visions and open viewers' minds to new and fresh outlooks. As phrased by Viktor Shklovsky, one of the founders of Russian formalism,

> art exists (so) that one may recover the sensation of life; it exists to make one feel things, to make the stone *stony* …. The technique of art is to make objects "unfamiliar," to make forms difficult, to increase the difficulty and length of perception because the process of perception is an aesthetic end in itself. *Art is a way of experiencing the artfulness of an object; the object itself is not important.* (1965: 12)

Another formalist precept concerns the conception of the relation of art to nature (i.e., Shklovsky's "object"). The best phrasing of this idea, although coming from art and film-as-art theorist and Gestalt psychologist Rudolph Arnheim, can be found in the following:

> There is a decisive difference between things of nature and works of art …. In the visual arts … form is applied to a material by external influence. In fact, the artist tends to avoid highly organized materials such as crystals or plants. The art of arranging flowers is hybrid because it subjects organic shape to human order …. Kracauer has pointed out that in photography highly defined compositional form falsifies the medium …. Artistic shape is made, whereas organic shape is grown …. The shape of a seashell or a leaf is the external manifestation of the inner forces that produced the object. (1967: 52–53)

Concomitant with the idea that art's general essence resides in the shaping of matter toward abstraction, many formalists maintained that each artistic medium has its own specific essence in that its abstracting formal devices develop from its specific means of production. As the Russian formalist Boris Kazanskij put it,

The specific properties of any art form whatever, we are taught by the contemporary science of art study, must be sought in its manner of execution, i.e. in its material technological basis. This in turn conditions both its entire system of devices and the full range of variations in its styles. (1981: 103)

Thus music shapes sounds toward abstraction through musical instruments, poetry shapes words through writing, painting shapes colors through brushes and canvas, and theater shapes the living, present human being through acting, stage, and decor. Attempts to shape the matter of one art form according to abstracting devices developed through the means of production of other arts were perceived by several formalists as alien to the art form: Trying to use compositions stemming from painting or poetry to shape the living human being in theater renders poor theater, just as trying to understand a play through the real history it alludes to renders a poor understanding of the play.

The advent of film generated a heated debate over its value as an art form. It brought forth a hidden dichotomy between these two widespread formalist premises concerning art's essence – namely, that each artistic form fashions its own peculiar materials, and that art strives toward abstraction. For the Russian formalists, art's struggle for abstraction was bound by definition to encounter strong resistance from the film's "material," given its technological, automatic, and highly mimetic way of recording reality. For them, the medium was anti-aesthetic according to its photographic-reproductive thrust and hence somewhat limited in its artistic potential. This position on film was most comprehensively detailed by Yuri Tynjanov, who saw film's aesthetic evolution as striving toward abstraction through overcoming its aesthetically debasing immanent faculty of reproduction. From this, Tynjanov reached the conclusion that the two main devices or "materials" specific to the art of film were the "cinematogenic" (i.e., the stylistic transmutation of objects within shots based upon the cine-camera's "distortions") and the montage (the "mounting" or editing of film shots). These devices shift the photographed object's naturalistic motivation toward an artistic one. Thus, while the cinematogenic shifts a figured object's meaning away from naturalistic motivations toward the film's internal artistic framework within the shot, montage stylistically interrelates the film shots, allowing for the "semantic correlativity of the visible world … rendered by means of its stylistic transformation" (Tynjanov 1981: 85). This idea of calculated style and composition was cardinal for art and film art as he instantiated it in literature by showing how in Gogol's short story *The Nose*, through a compositional and stylistic shaping of words, the reader accepts as plausible a nose that is detached from a body and can talk, think, and move around.

Tynjanov also maintained that film is art only insofar as it strives for abstraction and defamiliarization. Therefore, he held that mimetic or realist styling were artistically inferior since their composition was motivated by an attempt to mimic the shape of real things rather than by the artistic struggle toward formal abstraction. Particularly relevant to our concerns is Tynjanov's position on the story (*fabula*) in films, rejected because of the encouragement of the natural tendency of viewers to construct the film into a chronology of events with a beginning, middle, and end. He considered this narrative urge to stem from a realist rather than an aesthetic motivation, imposing thus standardized reality perceptions and concerns that obstruct estrangement, abstraction, and potential new outlooks. For him, attention to a chronological story construct distracts viewers away from the formal compositions which he rather saw embedded in what he called the plot (*sujet*). He suggested that the viewer's natural tendency to organize narrative data into a chronological story should be left unsatisfied and used at best to seduce the viewer into paying attention to the artwork's formal organization. As he elaborated, story is extraneous to the artwork whereas the plot is potentially artful since it entails the dynamic, moment by moment, formal and thematic patterning and weaving of the movie, including its contrived spatial, temporal, and causal (dis)organization. That is, the viewer's focus upon constructing the story out of the plot implies the reductive organization of the plot's abstractions and formal patterning into a real-life derived and non-artistic idea of a sequence with a beginning, middle, and end. As he put it, "Maximum emphasis on plot equals minimum emphasis on story and conversely" (ibid.: 100).[1]

Tynjanov therefore tended to support as virtuous films without stories or with poor ones, finding the 1920s films of the Russian revolutionary avant-garde filmmakers interesting. This, however, was not because of the communist revolutionary thrust that led them to search new forms to express new meanings, nor due to their propagandistically aimed poor story formation, but because this thrust and simple story structure or lack thereof led to interesting, abstract formal experimentation. Tynjanov's views can be related to Eisenstein's conflicting formal montage constructs as evidenced in the famous "Odessa Steps" sequence, forming along with other formally exploratory sequences the heavy-handed and propagandistic story of *Battleship Potemkin* (1925); to Vsevolod Pudovkin's similarly structured and simple story of *The Mother* (1926); or to Dziga Vertov's nonnarrative documentary *The Man with a Movie Camera* (1929), a film that offers often dazzling formal configurations that piece together brief documentary shots of daily life in the Soviet Union along with shots of the process of the film's shooting and editing.[2]

The early 1920s Russian formalist approach to film migrated to the West, influencing the re-emergence of formalism in film studies during the 1960s. This is particularly evidenced in the neoformalist work of Noël Burch on narrative films. Differing from Tynjanov, Burch did address narrative films with complex story structures, but he managed somehow to focus upon these films' formal configurations irrespective of their narrative thrust, implying that the themes of these movies can be comprehended from their formal system. Rather than dealing with the diachronic story structure of these films, Burch offers a meticulous synchronic analysis of several narrative films based on a typology of formal sound/image, space/ time, and off-/on-screen relations, in an attempt to outline actual and potential formal configurations (based on dialectical, or rather asymmetrical or contradictory, intra- or inter-shot formal interrelations). Through such formal analysis, Burch finds, for example in Michelangelo Antonioni's *Cronaca di un Amore* (Story of a Love Affair, 1950), a formal stylistics used, according to him, to articulate the theme of alienation through its playing, for example, with a character's intermittent inclusion or exclusion from a lengthy shot frame (1969: 27–28).

Before turning to the question of how formalism implies a notion akin to that of optional thinking I would like to discuss how formalist tenets inflected other perspectives on film, thereby also inflecting the latter's notions that are akin to optional thinking.

3.1.2. Formalist Influences on Other Perspectives

The advent of film brought forth a hidden dichotomy between the widespread formalist premises concerning art's essence—namely, that each artistic form fashions its own peculiar materials and that art strives toward abstraction. As we have seen, for the Russian formalists, art's struggle for abstraction was bound by definition to encounter strong resistance from the film's peculiar material, given its technological, automatic, and highly mimetic way of recording reality. For them, the medium was antiaesthetic due to its peculiar material, consisting of a photographic reproductive thrust, and hence somewhat limited in its artistic potential. Others, however, adhering to these same formalist principles, yet unable to dilute or dismiss this art form's peculiar material (i.e., its photographic ability to accurately visually reproduce the viewed reality), opted for a different approach. Thus, Rudolph Arnheim, somewhat countering his strict formalist position on the incompatibility between man-made and natural composition (see above), tried to strike a balance between film's formal two-dimensionality and its three-dimensional realist illusion, by suggesting that film art resided in this in-between situation, thus evoking a peculiar formal reflection on the nature of both art and life (Arnheim 1957). Andre Bazin, however, went to the illusionist pole in adhering to the first formalist premise rather than the second. Thus, in conceiving the filmic essential material to be the reproduction of reality, Bazin called for the development of a unique, "revelatory," aesthetic film realism whose main thrust was to uncover the world's beauty and minimize as much as possible the imposition of human formal configurations.

Some Frankfurt school Marxists, particularly Theodor Adorno, also took a favorable view of formalism in art in opposition to the dominant Marxist and neo-Marxist rejection of formalism on account of its depoliticization of art. Following his notion of "determinate negation" (Adorno 1997: 436) whereby the social prospects of art in Western capitalist society were proposed to be a dead end, Adorno considered the formalism-derived notion of art as pure formal play of abstraction to be a potential revolutionary "opening" of the mind for lack of viable alternatives (ibid.: 436).

Adorno's approach seems to have been espoused by Annette Michelson, the most formidable supporter of United States minimalist art and the related United States "pure film" movement of the 1960s. Michelson's notion of "film's radical aspiration" (Michelson 1970) as consisting of the experimental reconfigurations of time and space allowed by film's optical and editing faculties, potentially questioning thereby established perceptions and vision, suggests, as the title of an interesting paper on her work put it, using film as a "cognitive instrument in the service of revolutionary change" (Taylor 1992). However, differing from Adorno's predilection for abstract art, Michelson turned to consider the various ways in which, as Tynjanov put it, films, including narrative films, offer the "semantic correlativity of the visible world ... rendered by means of its stylistic transformation" (1981: 85). Following this line of thought, Michelson turned, among others, to study the works and writings of the revolutionary Soviet film avant garde (in particular the work of Vertov and Eisenstein) but also studied Stanley Kubrick's *2001: A Space Odyssey* (1968). In respect of the latter, an analysis of Kubrick's film shows how, in the use within the film of the figure of the impermeable black monolith, and in the visual conveyance of the lack of Cartesian coordinates when showing the spaceship's space flotation, the film manages to offer a "semantic correlativity" of a narrative dealing with humanity's cognitive evolution and ending with the proposition that humanity can bodily overcome spatial and temporal constraints.

Some film cognitivists, notably Bordwell, have also incorporated into their cognitive theory of how viewers comprehend films several formalist tenets, such as the idea of artistic motivation, cognitive reflexivity, and the interrelation of story, plot, and style. However, Bordwell included artistic or aesthetic motivation as one of several motivations viewers can ascribe to a given film configuration. He also seems to imply that artistic motivation is usually a default viewer strategy, simply meaning a semantically empty stylistic gesture used in case all other types of motivations that viewers can attribute fail (e.g., realist, generic). Also, Bordwell developed these formalist ideas in tackling the ways that narrative movies may engender reflexivity in viewers:

> In experiencing art [and popular film], instead of focusing on the pragmatic results of perception, we turn our attention to the very process itself. What is non conscious in everyday mental life becomes consciously attended to. Our schemata get shaped, stretched and transgressed; delay in hypothesis-confirmation can be prolonged for its own sake. (1985: 32)

However, contrary to formalists, this was carried out in respect of how the narrative articulation of the complex style, plot, and story may lead to such reflexive cognitive processes.

Finally, some postmodernists, notably Lev Manovich, have espoused formalist tenets. This is evidenced in Manovich's "data-base narratives" which he suggests to be the model underlying computer based "new media" works. By using Vertov's film *The Man with a Movie Camera* as paradigmatic precedent to the formal experimentation characterizing "new media," Manovich suggests a double formal articulation model. This model consists of a formally synchronic structure, within whose constraints, and based upon a given "data-base," different diachronic narrative trajectories ("algorithms") can be outlined. Thus, in his formalist analysis of Vertov's film, he suggests it is based upon a positioning of the processes of the film's production (e.g., shooting, editing, and screening) as the formally synchronic structure within whose constraints the film's various editing compilations of brief film shots construing its "data-base" are played out.

I will now turn to discuss these various formalist or formalist-influenced positions in respect of some of their ideas that are akin to optional thinking.[3]

3.1.3. Formalism and Optional Thinking
—a Failed Alternative

For formalists, as argued above, art's essence resides in the human abstraction of content through form, irrespective of the reality-based function of such a process (except, perhaps, sensitizing people to the formal qualities of the world surrounding them). What is important in art and in an artistic mentality as opposed to daily functional activities is that art draws attention to its forms. It does so by different devices "estranging" or defamiliarizing familiar objects from customary perceptions (e.g., a huge, oblique close up of one hair). In such manner, perceivers of art are forced to pay attention to the object's formation.

There are two major consequences most formalists derive from the notion of defamiliarization and its drawing of attention to form, consequences that may be taken to be akin to the encouragement of optional thinking. One is that such process leads perceivers to reflect on their mental processes "because the process of perception is an aesthetic end in itself" (Shklovsky 1965: 12). This Kantian idea of art as engendering mental reflection on perceptual and cognitive processes is very widespread[4] and as mentioned above, it also informs cognitive approaches to film, particularly as these have been elaborated in the work of David Bordwell. Thus, beyond other formalist influences Bordwell suggested that a film's violation of, or digression from viewers' expectations (concepts akin to "defamiliarization") as derived from their cognitive construction process of the story in their mind engenders in viewers awareness of processes such as the raising of hypotheses which are akin to the process of optional thinking.

However, I would argue that it is not clear from the formalist position (nor from Bordwell's) why, how, or under what circumstances "defamiliarization" (or digression from viewer expectations) and its attendant attention to formal patterning brings this about. Due to the fact that perception and an object's identification are made difficult, or that a film violates viewer-formed hypotheses, it does not follow that the perceiver is by necessity led to think about or contemplate in an inward manner, the perceptual or cognitive processes he/she is undergoing. This crucial, unexplained leap of logic has deep implications for the whole notion of reflexivity in art as somehow leading people to ponder upon *how* they think. I will not discuss this further because it goes beyond the confines of this book. I would simply suggest that inward reflection on thought processes requires particular mental attention to this and I do not see how such attention is necessarily evoked by defamiliarization and its attendant attention to form.

The second consequence is the most relevant to the issue of optional thinking. It can be found in Shklovsky's claim that art can "transfer the usual perception of an object into the sphere of new perception—that is, to make a unique semantic modification" (1965: 21). This cardinal idea was also stated by Tynjanov in his contention that the calculated stylistic exploitation of the necessary formal distortions of the photographed world (embedded, e.g., in shot angle, distance, framing, and shot assembly), achieved through the "cinematogenic" process of shooting and correlated through "montage," allows for the "semantic correlativity of the visible world ... rendered by means of its stylistic transformation" (1981: 85).

It is particularly in this idea that the formalist approach can be understood as heralding an earlier theory of optional thinking. Formalists conceive of attention to formal experimentation and patterning as the most viable artistic way to engender fresh and new outlooks: the calculated stylistic system of a film wrenches and transforms previous meanings ascribed to the contents or subjects addressed into the modified semantics brought forth by the stylistic system. Moreover, if this stylistic system is not concerned with mimicking standard reality perceptions, but is rather based on their stylistic "defamiliarization," then the semantic modification primarily modifies standardized modes of perception. Hence, it could be said that this strategy suggests optional thinking, at least in respect of a shift away from "standardized" ways of looking at the contents and subjects addressed in such films.

I would argue, however, that while optional thinking implies a "semantic modification," it is not clear from the formalist position why "defamiliarization" and its attendant attention to formal patterning is a privileged way to engender "fresh outlooks" or what is exactly meant by "semantic modification." Hence, semantic modification need not result necessarily from formal modification. That is, semantic modification may result from the articulation of different or contrasting points of view, both based upon a similar stylistic articulation. Moreover, formal modification that draws attention to form dilutes or subverts attention away from the modified content (e.g., the "object" in Shklovsky) or narrative (as suggested by Tynjanov). I would suggest that this process in itself may engender a *particular* semantic modification irrespective of the semantic modification that may be attained by not drawing exclusive attention to form. Hence, I suggest that it is most probably the case that enhanced attention to the formal process engendering semantic modification (whether through "defamiliarization" or not), at the cost of attention to the content or narrative modification (as is the case with the diminished attention to the content of sentences given as examples in grammar books), results in a particular conception of any such reached semantic modification as arbitrary—that is, always as a game-like, reduced modification. In other words, the attempt to generate a semantic modification by drawing attention to the formal process of modification, rather than the content or narrative being formally modified, results in a game-like or semantic modification that is perceived as arbitrary (see below a consideration of a possible fruitful direction for a disengagement of form from content).

The major problem with the formalist position rests in the belief that diverting attention away from either content (Shklovsky's "object") or narrative (Tynjanov, Burch) translates into fresh outlooks and meaningful (rather than game-like and arbitrary) semantic modifications. While Tynjanov seems to me to be correct when stating that in order to articulate a sustained semantics or to create a semantic modification you need a calculated style (see the mention above of his analysis of Gogol's *The Nose*), detaching style from, or highlighting it over, the content and narrative articulated, obstructs the comprehension of the semantics or of their modification. When in Woody Allen's *Sleeper* (1973) we accept that a dead leader's nose (kept in order to genetically reconstruct the leader) can be hijacked and have a gun pointed at it, we laugh at the ridiculous situation because it is feasible within the overall stylistic modification of the content of futuristic genetics, not because we are aware of the stylistic formal strategies that engender this event as feasible. Actually, were we to pay attention to how the style allows for such a ridiculous situation to become feasible, the joke would be lost on us, along with the option to standardize perception presented by this semantic modification.

The concomitant divorce of form from content implied in the notion of "defamiliarization" engenders split attention and distraction rather than enhanced and meaningful awareness toward *both* the process of semantic modification and the modified semantics. It does not seem to be the case that we can pay serious attention at the same time both to the forming of the object and to the resulting modification of the content. As Gombrich contended:

> We feed the information from the picture plane into the same kind of mill into which we also feed the information from the optic array. And because it is a mill, a process, an operation, it is not easy to halt. I would not say and never did say that we could not halt it up to a point, and view the picture plane as such. What I doubted and continue to doubt is that we can do both at the same time. We cannot, for the same reason that we cannot speak or write two different words at the same time. (Gombrich 1969: 65)

It is for this latter reason, namely, the split attention implied in paying simultaneous attention to both the form and the content/narrative illusion, a split that Shklovsky's and Tynjanov's heralded notion of "defamiliarization" by necessity creates, that "defamiliarization" fails as a viable way to evoke optional thinking. This is also why Arnheim's suggestion that viewers can maintain an in-between position in respect of the relation of the two-dimensional plane and the three-dimensional illusion, simultaneously reflecting on the formal aspects and on the fiction, is unfeasible. Finally, this is also why Manovich's sophisticated, double formal articulation fails to encourage optional thinking. In the latter case, this is because it implies a "double defamiliarization" of the content/illusion, both in respect of enhanced attention to the formally synchronic structure (e.g., Vertov's highlighted process of film production in *The Man with a Movie Camera*) and in the attention to the formal aspect of variation rather than the content of the variations (e.g., *The Man with a Movie Camera*'s various edited compilations of the brief film shots construing the film's "data-base").[5]

Furthermore, in explaining the relation of style to content/narrative, Gombrich clearly states that in such cases the content/narrative illusion overcomes the viewer's attention to the formal articulation. As he puts it:

> When we approach the problem of illusion ... the surface is irrelevant to our processing [of the object] and disappears from our awareness .... The perception of meaning [i.e., meaning of the object] can more easily be triggered than it can be eradicated, because it is automatic. When watching an exciting film we surely attend to the information rather than to the screen. The movie is altogether a good example of what I called automatic processing. We process the successive frames of the film as information about movement, and in this case we are quite unable to halt the automatism, which is partly physiological. We see movement, not a succession of stills, and similarly, I would maintain, we also see a man coming toward us rather than a configuration of shapes getting larger. The dark, of course, which blots out the screen helps to suppress the contradictory information presented by the surround; you can do the same with any painted picture if you screen off the frame and the wall with your hands or look at it through a tube. The distance of the painting surface will then be hard to establish and this will enhance the experience of depth. (Gombrich 1969: 55)

The position Gombrich advocates here, whereby in watching a film (particularly an "exciting" film) the illusion "takes over," should not be confounded with irrational notions of illusionism whereby the viewer somehow mistakes the image for reality. Carroll has widely discussed such irrational notions (e.g., N. Carroll 1996a: 367) while also providing a rational explanation for the power of cinematographic images. This power, he claims, resides in their superiority over other systems of pictorial representation since the movie camera is based upon the cultural invention (rather than convention) of perspective in painting, an invention that fits the way human vision perceives the world better than any other such system (N. Carroll 1988: 142–145). Therefore, while viewers do not consider for even a split second that what they see is real, they mostly attend to the content portrayed by the camera's powerful pictorial representation, given its tangible support of the fiction (particularly narrative fiction)—an attention that allows them to cognitively and emotively imagine the "what if?" situations and stories presented. In this respect, Bazin's theory of the cinematic illusion is irrational. His belief that a photographic or cinematic reproduction "shares, by virtue of the very process of its becoming, the being of the model of which it is the reproduction; it is the model" (1967a: 14) rests upon an irrational conflation of image and the object reproduced. Usually, such irrational conflations are not very productive for evoking viable processes of knowledge construction. This is indeed the case with Bazin's overlay of the conflation of the image and "the being" of the object with a predilection for ambiguous cinematic images, since these impart to the viewer the ambiguous nature of the reality whose "being" these images share. Thus, he conceives of his favorite deep-focused, long take to "reintroduce ambiguity into the structure of the image [: t]he uncertainty in which we find ourselves as to the spiritual key or the interpretation we should put on the film" (Bazin 1967b: 36). While this positioning of the viewer vis-à-vis the deep-focused image might imply an encouragement of the viewer to entertain alternatives, I contend that what interests Bazin is the uncertainty embedded in this ambiguity rather than the possible options emanating from it. Bazin, based upon an irrational conflation, offers an idealization and mystification of the ambiguity of reality. Far from conceiving of the deep-focused image as encouraging viewers to entertain options as to its meaning, Bazin lauds its apparent and always evasive mystery. Balazs, whose views are often akin to those of Bazin, has stated this position clearly in characterizing the close up of the human face as a site where "we can see there is something there that we can't see" (Balazs 1970: 76). Hence, Bazin's notion of how the deep-focused image positions the viewer implies mental rumination on the viewer's part rather than

optional thinking for knowledge construction, for it is based upon
a preconception of an ultimate undecipherable reality, transposed
by the deep-focused, ambiguous image onto the screen.

Gombrich's position on the primacy of the illusion carries a further implication for the formalist position insofar as optional thinking is concerned. Thus, when a calculated style is used to articulate a
new perception of the content or a narrative trajectory, as suggested
by Tynjanov, which is the usual case in most (stylistically cohering)
films, the illusion portrayed by such a style "takes over" and is not
consciously comprehended as resulting from the unique stylistic system. This is why, for example, while Burch's detection of the formal
configurations in Antonioni's *Cronaca di un Amore* may construe the
movie's theme of alienation differently from how it was previously
formed and perceived by viewers, the viewer comprehends and can
follow this theme coherently only by being nonconscious of the style
that creates this new or fresh understanding. If viewers would try to
follow this revised understanding by focusing their attention upon
the stylistic configuration, their attention would be split between the
deployment of the style and the theme of alienation that this style articulates, thereby obstructing their awareness of any fresh or optional
comprehension of the theme.

Once we concur with Gombrich's position, Michelson's revision
of Tynjanov's dictum whereby the "semantic correlativity of the visible world ... [as] rendered by means of its stylistic transformation"
can be used as a "cognitive instrument in the service of revolutionary change" has to be taken to mean that this cognitive revolutionary change is content bound. That is, for the viewer, the cognitive
and perceptual revolutionary change can be comprehended foremost as derived from the change in the content dealt with rather
than from awareness of the stylistic configuration. This is because
the stylistic configuration is inadvertent for a viewer entertaining
the fictional illusion. Thus, for the viewer, the altered perception is
bound to the content. Hence, I contend that Michelson's brilliant
detection of the formal strategies adopted, for example, by Kubrick
in *2001: A Space Odyssey*, in particular his shooting the spaceship
as floating in space, not located according to Cartesian coordinates,

may *not* be taken to imply that these formal strategies can change
the cognition of the viewers concerning the content of this film in a
revolutionary way. *2001: A Space Odyssey* suggests for most viewers
a new explanation of human evolution as being a result of cognitive
leaps. These leaps do not result from an orderly evolutionary path
but are effected by an unknown, alien entity (the black monolith)
that when touched advances their cognitive abilities: first, during
the stone age, humans realize upon touching the monolith that
they can use tools; and second, in the space age, upon touching the
mysterious monolith they are eventually freed from the constraints
of time and space. This transpires through showing the last astro-
naut left in the spaceship's odyssey encountering himself as an old
man, and in the film's ending, showing a fetus of a new human type
floating in space. Michelson's analysis of this movie seems to suggest
that the viewer's awareness of the possible change in human cognition and perception implied in the movie results primarily from the
viewer's attention to the formal strategies used. Furthermore, she
seems to imply that the formal rendering of the movie proposition
gears the viewer to assess it as an optional explanation for human
evolution vis-à-vis whatever the viewer's notion of human evolution
was before he entered the theater. We may presume that for Michelson, this reassessment stems from the difference between the film's
formal articulation of its proposition and the usual movie strategies
that inadvertent to the viewer forge the option that human bodies
are bound by Cartesian coordinates.

However, given Gombrich's argument espoused here, whereby
formal changes are inadvertent to the viewer (given the primacy
of the illusion), it becomes questionable whether the strategy of
shooting the spaceship in a way that does not conform to Cartesian
coordinates is what gears the viewer toward entertaining the movie's
proposition that the human body can be freed from space–time
coordinates. This is simply because *2001: A Space Odyssey's* formal
articulation, when necessarily viewed in respect of the content articulated, maintains a clear distinction between movement on earth
and in space in a manner that corresponds to, and supports the
viewer's regular understanding that in space-flotation, as opposed to

movement on earth, Cartesian coordinates do not apply. At most, Kubrick's formal articulation of space-flotation may lead the viewer to entertain or "feel" what it is like to float in space. This does not mean that had Kubrick used space-flotation style to articulate the movements of humans on earth his movie proposition would have been more seriously entertained by viewers. It simply means that forms cannot be dealt with irrespective of contents and that the contents predominate in any film's form-content mill.

The primacy of content in the viewer's perception and cognition of the movie obstructs formalist-oriented, implied notions that inadvertent formal configurations can engender viable optional thinking in viewers without forging a narrative content that compels the viewer to entertain the alternatives as viable. While a formal style inadvertent to the viewer may forge an optional way for seeing things, it cannot lead by itself to a change in the viewer's cognition or to optional thinking, since the viewer's attention is first and foremost given to the content and the narrative.

I would also like to address a cardinal issue concerning formalism by briefly discussing Adorno's notion of abstract art and its affinity to formalism as "determinate negation." I contend that Adorno's notion discussed above, whereby an art that resists any attempt at interpretation or signification can open the mind, cannot be divorced from the fact that such a claim itself is an act of meaning attribution, signification, and interpretation. At minimum, such interpretation demands a whole array of social conditions that may, or may not translate into this refusal of interpretation as constituting an act of resistance that may open people's minds. While abstract form may be discussed "in the abstract" (itself an act of interpretation), the most promising idea in such an approach is that it reveals that formal configurations may be applied to different contents, precisely because forms do not translate in and of themselves to such and such a meaning. True, formal configurations usually accumulate meanings by repetition, and it is often very hard to wrench these from such meanings. It is also true, however, that the meanings ascribed to certain formal configurations can, and often do mutate. My point, to be precise, is that forms have an autonomous existence from content and meaning in that they can be used to convey different contents and meanings. But from this it does not follow whatsoever that forms can be dealt with irrespective of contents or meanings.[6]

The formalist approach, in its predilection of form over content, context, and "a story with an end," while evoking for the initiated in the discourse surrounding abstract art some optional thinking in some nonnarrative artworks, is simply besides the point when discussing narrative films in terms of optional thinking. In cases where such an approach guides the perception of narrative films, it may at best evoke occasional decontextualized and localized optional thinking. This is because applying this approach to narrative movies while dismissing or underplaying their most pertinent quality— that is, the edited, flowing, audiovisual formation of content within the context of narration and storytelling, imposes a reflexive working "against the grain" (i.e., narrative) that pushes and pulls perception toward and away from narrative, engendering split attention and its attendant distraction. Conversely, when the reflexive formal thrust works with the narrative, it conceives the formal configurations by necessity in the context of the content articulated and the narrative thrust, along with the anticipation evoked by narrative and the expectancy for a cohering trajectory. Thus, when attention to formal configuration is reflexively experienced within the context of narrative articulation it does not engender optional thinking due to the immanent form–content conflation imposed by narrative. Conversely, when working against the grain, reflexive thought is hard to sustain and renders at best occasional optional thinking and at worst, split attention, distraction, or boredom.

I suggest that only under certain terms formal configurations may raise optional thinking. This might occur when a style that has accumulated a distinct ambiance and meaning (as in generic styles such as that of musicals or westerns with their respective "life is music" or "civilization vs. nature" semantics) is made explicit by drawing attention to the meaning accumulated by the stylistic/formal configuration, and if this attention to a meaningful style alternates with attention to a narrative (illusion) that constructs a story whose locale, subject matter, and contents do not pertain to that associated with the style deployed. In this case we may presume that the viewer effectively faces two different semantic trajectories that he can compare (rather than a semantic-narrative trajectory and a formally abstract trajectory that articulates it). Under such circumstances, and only if these two diverging (narrative vs. formal-with-accumulated-meaning) semantic trajectories are interrelated in such a manner that the viewer needs to consider both as different interpretative options for the subject matter at hand, we may assume that optional thinking is encouraged. In chapter 4 I will discuss the emergent yet problematic deployment of such a strategy in Quentin Tarantino's use of the western genre in *Inglourious Basterds* and Lars von Trier's use of the musical genre in *Dancer in the Dark* (2000).

3.2. The Neo-Marxist Approach: Narrative Deconstruction

The second major approach to movies engendering something akin to optional-thinking deficiency is the influential, neo-Marxist, Althusser-derived approach to film (e.g., Baudry 1985; Dayan 1976; Heath 1981).

Neo-Marxists critiqued formalism for its disregard of content. They claimed that their heralding of abstract formal experimentation on account of an impossible detachment from content and (social) context was not only futile but actually engendered asocial feelings and thereby supported political systems interested in social apathy. Burch himself critiqued, in retrospect, "the source of embarrassment" of his early work as: "Formalism. A formalism of the worst kind …[:] flight from meaning …[;] a neurotic rejection of 'content' [which] stemmed from a studied ignorance, and fear of the political" (1981: vi). For neo-Marxists, with the notable exception of some members of the Frankfurt School such as Adorno (see above), formalism was anti-revolutionary and served capitalist ideology or even supported fascist politics. As it is succinctly put by Walter Benjamin, "'Fiat ars – pereat mundus' says Fascism …. This is evidently the consummation of 'l'art pour l'art' [i.e., formalism]

.... This is the situation of politics which Fascism is rendering aesthetic. Communism responds by politicizing art" (1969: 242).

However, while neo-Marxists attacked formalism for its focus upon abstract form on account of attention to content and context, they too gave particular attention to formal configurations based on the idea succinctly put by neo-Marxist film director Jean Luc Godard's idea, that if you want to say something different you have to say it differently. Hence, while both formalists and neo-Marxists paid particular attention to form, they differed in that neo-Marxists considered forms to carry an ideological import.[7]

This focus upon the ideological import of formal configurations led different neo-Marxist film scholars to consider movies as engendering something akin to closed mindedness. Their response to this has taken the form of deconstruction. The strategy of deconstruction may be considered as implying something akin to the encouragement of optional thinking in viewers but, as I will argue, overall, neo-Marxism and films influenced by this approach offer a failed alternative to the encouragement of optional thinking.

3.2.1. Neo-Marxist Tenets

A central concern of neo-Marxists in the capitalist "First World" was the apparent failure of Marx's prediction that a world proletarian revolution would occur by necessity, given the relentless expansion of the brutal, capitalist mode of production. Stalin's policy of the containment of socialism to the Soviet bloc and the growing strength of capitalism in the West led them to consider the factors that impeded a communist revolution in the West. Antonio Gramsci (Gramsci 1971) developed the idea that capitalism's survival derives foremost from the superstructural cultural-political hegemony of the ruling classes. No social order, he maintained, can survive without social legitimacy based upon a broad social consent. He therefore reached the conclusion that capitalism persists not because it is not materially exploitative or brutal but because the ruling classes manage to persuade the ruled classes that the mode of production exploiting them is natural and even desirable. In his view, changes in the material base structure that should lead to revolution do not find expression in the superstructure because the cultural-political hegemony of the ruling classes brainwashes the minds of the exploited masses. A similar conclusion was reached by members of the Frankfurt School, whose critical theory maintained that the widespread popular culture in the capitalist West was a culture industry pumping capitalist ideologies into the heads of the exploited. This neo-Marxist approach was developed into a solid and very influential theory of ideology during the 1960s by French philosopher Louis Althusser.

According to Althusser, Marxism undervalued the autonomous functioning of ideologies and understood them "like the … dream among writers before Freud" (1971a: 159), that is, as a weightless reflection of material changes. Therefore, he claimed that Marxists wrongly maintained that changes in the base structure lead by necessity to homologous superstructural changes. In "Ideology and Ideological State Apparatuses" (Althusser 1971a), Althusser claimed that Marxism overlooked the function of the superstructure in thwarting the revolutionary process and in enabling the continuation of the exploitative, capitalist mode of production. He therefore set out to explain how this occurs. He reached the conclusion that this happens because of the superstructural "state apparatus," which coordinates between repressive state apparatuses and ideological ones. While repressive apparatuses (police, army, censorship, courts, jails, etc.) maintain the social order through force, ideological ones (the education system, the mass communication system, including movies, the family institution, etc.) do so by persuasion (ibid.: 143). He seems to have maintained that without effective ideological apparatuses the social order would collapse and revolution would ensue, implying that this would occur because repression by force would intensify, given the growing unrest of the exploited masses. Therefore, Althusser reached the conclusion that the major factor thwarting revolution is the ideological state apparatus that persuades the exploited masses that the mode of production exploiting them is right, necessary, and even desirable. Hence, as long as these apparatuses remain, there will be no need for the forceful repression that will hasten revolution. Having reached this conclusion, Althusser searched for the mechanism by which ideologies persuade people to operate against their material interests. He started by rejecting widespread definitions of ideology, in particular the claim that it is a twisted representation of reality. Hence people say of others that "they represent reality to themselves in a twisted manner" or, often when speaking of their past, they say, "I used to have a twisted representation of reality but now I see things clearly." Why, he asked, would people represent to themselves their reality in a twisted manner if they assume by that very definition that reality can be represented in a straightforward manner? His reply to this question was that these definitions of ideology fail because they are based on the misleading presumption that people can choose how to represent their reality. He reached the conclusion that ideologies are not chosen but given to people and that their persuasive power derives from the illusion they give people that they have chosen to believe in the reality depicted by a given ideology and that henceforth they are the ones constituting this ideological representation of reality of their own free will. Hence, concluded Althusser, ideologies operate by twisting the relation that people have to their reality, a twisting related to the illusion of choice (ibid.: 162–165). This illusion is what allows for ideological persuasion since if people perceive the ideology given to them as their own choice, they willingly submit to its representation of reality and willingly perform the duties it imposes upon them.

According to Althusser, the means by which people are manipulated into a fake notion of "choice" is their fake constitution as subjects. The concept of the subject, he said, aptly has a double meaning: on the one hand it refers to someone who is free to choose and take decisions; while, on the other hand it implies submission, the state of being subjected to something or someone else (as when we speak of a king's subjects) (ibid.: 182). Hence, ideology, any ideology, operates by *constituting concrete individuals as subjects*" (ibid.: 171). In fact, said Althusser, from the moment we have selfhood we are "always-already subjects" (ibid.: 176) of this or that ideology. In order to explain the conflation of subject and self Althusser relied on the theory of selfhood developed by the psychoanalyst Jacques Lacan (Althusser 1971c; Lacan 1977). Lacan hypothesized that a human's first notion of self results from his/her seeing themselves reflected in other humans or, wherever available, in their mirror image. Hence, he argued that between the ages of six and eighteen months, when human motor coordination lags behind a well developed sense of sight, the child identifies his/her reflection in others or in mirrors as separate, independent, whole, coordinated, and constant. The gap or contradiction between this initial identification with our reflected image and our deficient co-ordination, perceived as lack, is what determines our relation to selfhood throughout our lives. Hence, we will strive throughout our lives to fill this felt gap between our inner sense and the full image appearing in our outer self-reflection. According to Lacan, this is also the basis for our imaginary identification with others. Of particular importance for Althusser was that this initial sense of self is based upon a reflection in our minds of a detached image that does not correspond to our sensed material referent. Althusser's claim was that ideology, in its appealing to our selves, reconstitutes in us the sense of this imaginary self and suggests that we can attain fullness if, as "free", dependent subjects, we "choose" to emulate the fuller ideal Subject (with capital *S*) offered by an ideology (ibid.: 181). In turn, our identification with this imaginary ideal Subject suggests that if we strive to see the world from its point of view we will attain the desired fullness in our lives. In turning individuals into subjects through their notion of selfhood, ideology performs a reversal whereby people's material existence becomes abstract while their ideological imaginary becomes their reality (ibid.: 175).

Ideology operates by turning individuals into subjects, thus persuading them that it is out of their own free choice that a given production mode operates. In this manner ideology twists the relation individuals have to their real conditions of existence. Rather than viewing their position in society as imposed upon them, they believe that they have chosen to be there. This conception, attributing to dominant ideological apparatuses a cardinal role in the preservation of the capitalist mode of production, led Althusser to call for the deconstruction of ideologies through the deconstruction of the ideological processes constituting the subject.

3.2.2. Film as an Ideological Apparatus

Neo-Marxist film theoreticians and filmmakers were highly influenced by Althusser's theory of ideology. Viewing film as an ideological apparatus, they tried to discover how films turn viewers into their subjects and hence persuade them not only that the reality portrayed is a desired one, but that this reality could not exist without their own constitution of it. Jean Louis Baudry, for example, searched for the "Ideological Effects of the Basic Cinematographic Apparatus" (1985). His claim was that the invention of film derived from modern capitalism's need to reinstate in people the illusion of their having control over their own lives, an illusion needed for their willing cooperation with a mode of production that in fact has stolen away any remains of such self-control. Hence, he found in the film apparatus itself ideological effects that constitute a "transcendental"-centered subject (ibid.: 536–538), presumably therefore willing to cooperate with the capitalist mode of production. Following others he argued that the camera lenses, based as they were on the fifteenth-century Renaissance invention of linear perspective, adapted the ideological effects of this invention to modern capitalism. Hence, Leon Battista Alberti's invention of linear perspective (*perspectiva artificialis*) renders an illusion of three-dimensionality by organizing the space of a painting within a rectangular frame so that the overall line directions converge into one point, which Alberti termed the "vanishing point." The location of this point in the canvas converges with that of the eye level of a presumed-average spectator from whose point of view the painting is to be observed (ibid.: 532). Thus, a spectator who assumes the position prescribed by the painting, whereby his/her eye overlays the painting's vanishing point, experiences the full illusion of depth. According to Baudry, this deployment has a clear ideological effect since, in ideological terms, the painting organizes a homogenous, centered, and hierarchically organized space that appears to emanate from one originating point or to converge into it. This originating point is that of the painting's ideal viewing subject, whose point of view a spectator assumes. In such a manner the painting whose perspective is centered on the vanishing point constitutes its spectator as subject: S/he is positioned at a certain point that lets him/her experience themselves as the point to which all the illusory deep space converges, or as the origin from which it emanates (ibid.: 534). Baudry went on to claim that the cine-camera, based on linear perspective, enhances this ideological effect of subject transcendence since the cine-camera's point of view, which the viewer identifies as his own, can float over a continuously perceived deep space (a moving continuity itself achieved by the film projector's speed fooling the viewer's eye into not perceiving the discreetness of the still photographs that constitute the film strip) (ibid.: 536–537).

Given this, Baudry and others such as Dayan (1976: 446–449) and Heath (1981: 38–39) contended that editing the film shots together carries a potential subversion of the ideological effects of the camera lenses and the filmstrip projection, since each shot transition may make the viewer aware of the fact that the reality depicted is not under his/her control and that someone or something else is changing the setup. This potential subversion was, according to them, what motivated the evolution of continuous editing. In their view, continuous editing, whose main function is to hide shifts in camera positioning from the viewer's attention, ends up reinforcing the film's ideological effects. In order to ground this conclusion, Baudry enlisted the phenomenological philosophy of Edmund Husserl (537–538). Husserl's phenomenology (1999: 17–25) describes a thought process that can offer a viable explanation for the way in which continuity editing consolidates the position of the viewer as ideological subject. According to Husserl, since our sense data provide us with mere segments of a sensed object at any given time (e.g., we cannot simultaneously see an object's front and back), we derive our sense of selfhood from the partial

data provided by our senses because something has to deduce the
object's fullness as it appears in our mind. That something, said
Husserl, cannot but be our selfhood. Therefore, concludes Husserl,
the moment we constitute the object is the moment we constitute
our selves. Baudry used Husserl's theory to explain how continuity
editing, in its way of chaining together the partial data provided
by shot segments, reinforces rather than subverts the viewer's sense
of selfhood by easing the viewers' constitution of the film into a
coherent whole, thus implanting the ideological illusion that she is
the one constituting these film segments into a whole and by that
reinforcing her fake sense of selfhood and concomitant subjection
to the film's ideology (1985: 538). A similar approach to editing,
as potential subversion of ideology that is turned into its reinforce-
ment by continuity editing, was suggested by Dayan and Heath
(1981). Dayan (1976), concerned with the ideological effects of
continuity-editing transitions on the viewer, focused on the "shot–
reverse shot" construct, claiming it to be based on the "suturing"
of the viewer's consciousness into the film (447). Shot–reverse shot
constructs consist, for example, of a sequence in which the viewer
watches character B from the point of view of character A, followed by a shot showing the reverse angle in which A is seen from
B's point of view (and so on). Dayan claimed that in the first shot
(showing character B) the viewers fully identify with the camera's
point of view and sense themselves as originating the image. However, in the transition to the reverse shot the imaginary continuity
may be broken due to the change in camera angle and figuration,
potentially raising in the viewers' minds the question of who is
showing them the event, a question threatening to lay bare the film
apparatus and destroy the illusion and the spectators' attendant joy-
ful empowerment. However, according to Dayan, the shot–reverse
shot construct manipulates the potential raising of such a question
to serve its needs. This is because the reverse shot offers a retroactive
answer to the viewer's tacitly emergent question, whereby it was
character A that was watching character B. Thus the film diverts the
answer to the viewer's question from the level of the film apparatus
(i.e. the question raises the awareness to how the film is made) to

the fictional level (ibid.: 448–449), suggesting something like, "it was the character that you see now that was watching the character you just saw." Through such manipulations (termed by Dayan "the tutor code of cinema"), viewers' minds are "sutured" into the film and their illusionary empowerment is not only reinstated but reinforced (ibid.: 450). Heath expanded Dayan's theory. In "Narrative Space" (Heath 1981) he focused on what he termed a "narrativization process" that centers cinematic space around the action, thus generating an apparently continuous flow by bridging/suturing and thus incorporating into the enclosed composition of scenes and of the film as a whole the gaps opened in the editing process (ibid.: 43–45). Likewise, he maintained that the often deviant-from-realist generic stylistic variations that draw attention to film form (e.g., the conventions of the musical) and even to the film apparatus (e.g., autonomous camera movements offering realist-impossible points of view) are also incorporated as meaningfully empty stylistic devices whose disrupting potential serves to better affirm the overall wholesome, meaningful, cohering, narrative film flow (ibid.: 49–50). As it is put by Heath:

> Space comes in place through procedures such as look and point-of-view structures, and the spectator with it as subject in its realization …. The suturing operation is in the process, the give and take of absence and presence …. Narrativization, with its continuity, closes, and it is that movement of closure that shifts the spectator as subject in its terms: the spectator is the *point* of the film's spatial relations—the turn, say, of shot to reverse shot—their subject-passage. Narrativization is scene and movement, movement and scene, the reconstruction of the subject in the pleasure of that balance (with genres as specific instances of equilibrium)—for homogeneity, containment. What is foreclosed in the process is not its production … but … the outside—heterogeneity, contradiction, history—of its coherent address. (ibid.: 54)

According to these neo-Marxist film scholars, films, through "centered" audiovisuals and narratives leading to a single closure, constantly "suture" editing and stylistic gaps opened in the overall audiovisual narrative flow so as to "re-center" their viewers, thereby turning them back into the "subjects" they "always already" are. This notion of a centered subject, based on what they conceive as a false notion of self identity and an attendant fictive freedom of choice, is what allows in their view the manipulation of viewers into believing that they have chosen, and even control the constitution of the specific ideology imposed upon them in a narrative film. It is in this sense that this approach can be said to claim that movies impose on viewers closed mindedness; that is, in their imposing a single mode of viewing and comprehension that impedes the viewer's entertainment of alternatives to the ideology and point of view outlined in the movie.

3.2.3. Neo-Marxism and Optional Thinking —a Failed Alternative

Following Althusser, the conclusion reached by neo-Marxist film scholars and filmmakers was that there was a dire need to deconstruct the subject-positioning process of the film apparatus, so as to subvert its manipulation of viewers into a willing acceptance of, and desire to emulate the ideological reality screened before them. In their view, this could be achieved primarily by deconstructing the illusion of continuity, centeredness, and the visual/narrative coherence constructed by films and thereby constituting viewers as ideological subjects. They presumed that once the viewer becomes aware of these manipulations through such deconstruction, the film will lay bare its ideological manipulations and lose its ideological power. Thus, for Baudry, not allowing the viewer to construct a coherent world or narrative out of the film segments would result, according to his presentation of Husserl's phenomenology, in the viewer's incapability to assert his identity as subject. Likewise, for Dayan and Heath, disrupting the shot–reverse shot construct will lead the viewer to lose the illusion of control and derail the suturing process. Heath takes Nagisa Oshima's film *Death by Hanging* (1968) to instantiate his claims. *Death by Hanging* tells the story of R, a murderer sentenced to death, who has lost his identity after surviving his execution. Since R does not know who he is, he cannot be executed again until he regains his sense of identity, for otherwise he cannot be held responsible. The film follows the attempts of "correction officers" to help R regain his identity so that he can be executed again. However, according to Heath, the film's narrative problematization of the concept of the legal subject through R's amnesia destabilizes the viewer's notion of identity not because of its narrative subject matter, but because of Oshima's disjointed articulation, which breaks continuity and uses impossible camera angles as well as other strategies that make it difficult for the viewer to unify and make coherent the film's spatial, temporal, and narrative schemes. This deconstructive approach in filmmaking was most fully proposed in the work of Jean Luc Godard, whose dictum "if you want to say something different you have to say it differently" generated an impressive body of work, including the films *Masculine/Feminine* (1966), *Made in USA* (1966), *La Chinoise, 2 ou 3 choses que je sais d'elle* (Two or Three Things I Know About Her, 1967), and *Week End* (1968). Godard's films constantly destroy character, narrative, and temporal and spatial coherence. This is coupled with a deconstructive analysis of shots and sequences in the dominant cinema style, laying bare their presumed ideological manipulations of beauty and of human emotions. This is often complemented with a voiceover offering Marxist analyses of the social structure in the capitalist world and its resulting cinematic image of reality. For instance, in *La Chinoise*, a film critically dealing with the confused and mistaken naïve ideology of a Parisian Maoist group of youngsters, there is a scene where the characters play a romantic musical score on a gramophone to accompany the repetition of a conversation on the politics of language they have just had. In this scene, Godard not only makes the viewers conscious of film form and technique as formalists would have it, but he primarily lays bare how dominant cinema manipulates our emotions by showing how a political conversation loses its explicit meaning and changes into a romantic, emotional, subtextual interchange once the musical score is added. In another shot, showing a symmetrically arranged French bourgeois living room, dialectically opposed graffiti written on the wall reads: "We need to fight ambiguous words with clear images," thus apparently deconstructing the dominant cinema's manipulation of composition and beauty to promote its worldview.

As implied above, neo-Marxists suggested a decentered film articulation focused upon a deconstruction of centered articulations that, as put by Heath (1981: 33) when writing on Vertov, "would challenge that [subject-centering] vision by constructions of dissociations in time and space that would produce the contradictions of the alignment of [e.g.,] camera-eye and human eye in order to displace the subject-eye of the socio-historical individual into an operative – transforming – relation to reality."

It is in this latter sense that neo-Marxists may be said to suggest how films can evoke optional thinking. That is, through a deconstruction that lays bare the ideological machinations of a narrative film edited above all for continuity, the viewer is split or decentered as subject, thus presumably engendering in him/her "an operative – transforming – relation to reality." Moreover, as evidenced in Oshima's and Godard's films, when this deconstructive articulation is of a narrative whose subject matter is capitalist ailments (*Death by Hanging*) or is also intermittently interspersed by a metanarrative that addresses in an analytical manner the ailments of capitalism and their leading to ideological manipulations (e.g., *La Chinoise*), the expected viewer's "transforming relation to reality" is given an apparently viable neo-Marxist alternative course to the nontransforming relation-to-reality option embedded in a regular movie narrative.

For these Althusserian neo-Marxists, what is of major importance for the evocation of the described optional thinking is less the anticapitalist content of these films and more the stuttered, decentered articulation of the options' overlay. This is because what bothers them most is the "centered" subject. Thus, articulating in a coherent manner any of the options, including that of the neo-Marxist narrative or nonnarrative analytical discourse on society, would end up turning viewers into centered subjects, given the presumed ideological implications of any film's discourse as coherent (be it narrative or not).

It is this idea of the mutual, discursive deconstruction of options, insofar as it implies defying closed mindedness or evoking optional thinking, that I want to critique. I argue that what such deconstructive strategies imply is actually the deconstruction of the knowledge-construction process for viewers. Hence, deconstructing continuity and narrative coherence and closure carries with it by necessity the deconstruction of causality and the process of this causality leading to a conclusion in narratives. While, as I have claimed in chapter 1, this process in movies encourages closed mindedness and an apparent sense of strict causality, its deconstruction simply undermines the necessary narrative conditions for any process of knowledge construction and acquisition to ensue. That is, this deconstructive approach impedes the process in narratives that is akin to knowledge construction, thus preventing viewers from comprehending the film. The same goes for the occasional attendant nonnarrative, neo-Marxist analyses of the deconstructed narrative as used in Godard's films. This is so because while some such intermittent analyses may be comprehensible at certain junctures in the film, the viewer is pulled and pushed between the task of trying to construct the disjointed narrative and the required attention to such intermittent analytical interventions. This is somewhat comparable to someone listening simultaneously to two overlapping, different languages, each articulated in a stuttered manner. While he/she may understand each language separately, the mix and the stuttering engender split attention and miscomprehension. While in such films, occasional localized optional thinking may arise (as in the gramophone scene discussed above), it does not add up to a viable or even comprehensible optional trajectory. It simply leaves the viewers with a vague notion of what the film is about.

Moreover, while optional thinking implies the consideration of viable alternatives, for Althusserians any such alternative turns into nothing more than another ideological manipulation insofar as it is articulated through the centering strategies characterizing narrative films, or, for that matter, from any coherent articulation, since these alternatives are comprehended through the prism of the discursively constructed, self-identical, "centered" viewer-as-subject. This dead-end conception arises from Althusser's position on art in general, a position replicated by his followers in film whereby all that art can offer us is knowledge of effects on the workings of ideology (Althusser 1971b). Therefore, as long as the subject is "centered" by the film narrative discourse there are no meaningful alternatives (actually, according to Althusser, whether we watch films or not, we are "always already" subjects within the capitalist mode of production and its attendant false ruling ideology of individual freedom of choice).[8]

Whether this approach to individuals living under capitalism describes our predicament or not, the primary aim of deconstructing and dismantling the discursive machinations of film narratives, thus impeding the viewers' efforts to construct the narrative in their minds so as to dismantle their inner sense of "unity," is senseless and aimless. Hence, not only is it farfetched to assume that failure to perform this task of comprehension by viewers can in itself elicit a subject-unity fissure or split, it is also unclear why splitting the subject leads a split viewer to entertain an "operative – transforming – relation to reality" rather than, say, an inoperative, confused relation to it. That is, it is questionable whether splitting the subject is more of a desired outcome than the notion of a free self (presumed as fictive by Althusserians).

The neo-Marxists' approach seems to have failed even on its own terms. Thus, the ascent of postmodernism to cultural dominance during the 1980s and its overall presupposition of an inherently split subject challenged the viability of neo-Marxist theories of subject deconstruction. The attributes of the postmodern text segmentation and spatial or temporal decentering—based as they were on the presumption that subjects are split to begin with—led Jameson to the conclusion that contrary to neo-Marxist aspirations, what he perceived as the postmodern actual crumbling of the imaginary ideal subject did not lead to the release of a revolutionary mentality as hoped for by Althusser and his followers. Rather, it led to people losing identity and direction, and experiencing life through reified, disjointed moments. Lost in the postmodern "schizophrenic" maze, maintained Jameson, humans fail to cohere time, space, and identity, experiencing the incoherent moments of their lives as a series of temporary and shallow spectacles. Desires and memories are experienced as intense, reified, sensual excitements or as exchangeable objects that can be bought and sold. These processes he found expressed in nostalgic films alluding to an intangible past,[9] in dazzling cinematic spectacles lacking depth or logic, or in television where advertising structures an endless flow of images. Hence, Jameson called for a cognitive remapping of the social, economic, political, and cultural terrains for the redirection and reorientation of people caught in the global maze of globalizing capitalism (Jameson 1991: 95). In other words, Jameson can be said to have called for narrativization in the sense that this process couches events within a causal trajectory offering a sense of direction, suggesting that postmodernism's shattering of hierarchies and boundaries between high and low art, its leveling of different styles and historical periods, and its understanding of the text as an intersection of endless textual references do not lead to more real freedom and equality. He reached the conclusion that the cultural pluralism of the postmodern text was not a progressive expression of changes in the basic superstructure, but rather a regressive, superstructural expression of the base structure of globalizing capitalism. To paraphrase Walter Benjamin's view on fascism, it can be said that postmodernism is a new strategy to allow the masses cultural expression without serving their real, material interests. As I have claimed elsewhere, in Marxist terms, the shifting late-capitalist, global, decentered configurations of exploitation are actually supported by postmodern, superstructural, ideological and textual decentering strategies. These level and mix various positions, whereby the potent ones appear as yet another unprivileged position among others, all being apparently even.[10]

In sum, the neo-Marxist Althusserian approach to films, while pointing out some of the strategies through which popular narrative films engender closed mindedness, based as it is on a faulty notion of subject centeredness, fails in its deconstructive approach to offer a way for films to engender viable optional thinking. This failure also concerns the viewers' meaningful and complete comprehension of the alternative neo-Marxist ideas on film and society.

3.3. The Postmodern Approach: Simulacra, Intertextuality, Split Subjects, and Loopy Thinking

A third major approach to movies as encouraging something akin to closed mindedness is the postmodern one. Following a presentation of the tenets of this approach and the resulting consideration of narrative movies as a priori failed attempts to generate something akin to closed mindedness in viewers, the chapter considers how the postmodern notion of intertextuality may be taken to imply optional thinking. It will suggest that overall, postmodernism and most films influenced by it offer a failed alternative to the encouragement of optional thinking. This is because of the inherently self-contradictory notion of "open" intertextuality and the presupposition of a split subject. Thus, many films oriented by this approach are either incomprehensible or game-like, or encourage cognitive closure upon nonclosure and its attendant Sisyphus-style loopy thinking.

3.3.1. Postmodern Tenets

3.3.1.1. Simulacra

While neo-Marxists of the 1970s critiqued film formalism for abstracting reality and film realism for mystifying it, they shared with these approaches the presumption that reality is out there and that films ideologically react to it. This long held presumption came under attack with the advent of the postmodern episteme in the 1970s. Some postmodernists suggested that "reality" is nothing but models or simulations that generate whatever is defined by them as "reality." As Baudrillard described it, "the empirical object, to which qualities of shape, color, matter, function, and discourse are assigned ... is a myth ...[;] it is nothing but the types of relations and different meanings converging and swirling around it" (1981: 155). This postmodern perception gradually invaded different disciplines. Hence, historian Hayden White rejected the historians' pretension to reveal humanity's past through historical facts. Facts are in his view nothing more than texts that mediate an always-already mediated reality. The historian, rather than dealing with facts in an attempt to reveal an elusive past, constructs this past to begin with according to the structuring possibilities allowed by language or other communicative systems such as film (White 1978). A similar revolution occurred in the conception of scientific research when the philosopher of science Thomas Kuhn argued that scientists are driven in their research by a set of conventions and institutional directives (Kuhn 1970). Contrary to positions on scientific research such as that of Karl Popper (whose ideal was the search for truth through constant attempts at refuting scientific hypotheses, claiming that the more a hypothesis poses conditions that may lead to its refutation the more scientific it is), Kuhn contended that the evolution of scientific research is characterized by the upholding of theories until there is so much contradicting data that it becomes impossible to cling on to them. Moreover, claimed Kuhn, there is no assurance whatsoever that the new theory is any better than the one it replaced. The radical questioning of our ability to know the world was furthered by Michel Foucault's position that the search for truth is in itself nothing more than a powerful discourse competing with other discourses within the cultural configurations of power. There is not one truth, claimed Foucault, only discursive truisms (Foucault 1984). For Baudrillard in particular there seemed to be no "external" reality or truth at all. Hence, argued Baudrillard, it is not the case that somewhere beyond our faculties there is a reality mediated to us by images, but rather that reality is an image, that it is nothing but simulacrum. In "Simulacra and Simulations" he argued that the simulacrum, which was always present yet obscured, gradually came to the fore. Whereas earlier the image was discussed in terms of its reproducing or distorting a reality that presumably preceded it, today it seemed clear that all those early presuppositions were untenable mental manipulations aimed, through the constitution of fake hierarchies among different types of simulations, at foreclosing the fact that reality does not exist.

This approach seems to have influenced the turn of much documentary filmmaking toward what are termed "mockumentaries," that is, films that blur the distinction between fact and fiction. In rejecting the assumption that reality exists beyond human perception and can be revealed (realists) or must be departed from (formalists), postmodern filmmakers presumed from the outset that documentary and fiction are cultural categories or kinds of discourse with different styling whose distinction does not stem from their approach to an elusive prerecorded reality. Hence, postmodern films inadvertently and seamlessly mix documentary and fiction. Deliberate documentary-style lies and fictional truisms abound. For example, in Israeli filmmaker Avi Mugrabi's 1997 film *Eich Hefsakti Lefached ve'lamadeti le'ehov et Arik Sharon* (How I Learned to Overcome My Fear and Came to Love Arik Sharon), the director mixes a documentary following Ariel Sharon's election campaign with a deceitful documentation of both his slow transformation into one of Sharon's devotees and a fake presentation of the deterioration of his marital relations, ending with his wife's decision to leave him because of his changed political affiliation. A similar shift toward the status of reality can be evidenced in fiction films. *The Matrix* (Andy and Larry Wachowski 1999), for example, tells the story of a computer hacker who learns from mysterious rebels that reality is only a huge simulation, explicitly referencing Baudrillard when the film's protagonist Neo (Keanu Reeves) is seen with a copy of Baudrillard's "Simulacra and Simulation." The farfetched nature of the film's idea that the reality experienced by humans is nothing but a simulation, programmed by machines who suck through this simulation the human energy they need to keep their underworld going, ends up implying that neither world nor underworld are more than a simulation. Furthermore, the film's stunning digital effects make tangible the idea of reality-as-simulation through Neo's gradual empowerment to manipulate it by floating within it or by slowing, accelerating, or elasticizing it.

This relation between the digital revolution and Baudrillard's concept of the simulacrum has often been noticed by researchers. Hence, Vivian Sobchack suggested that the digital device of morphing instantiates Baudrillard's simulacrum in that the morph has no origin whatsoever, since that from which it changes does not "cause" or precede that to which it has changed (Sobchack 2000). The morph implies seamless reversibility and one image is not more real, original, or essentially different from the other. For instance, she recapitulates Baudrillard's ideas in a comparison she makes between the pre-morph film transformations in a montage sequence from *All that Jazz* (Bob Fosse 1979), showing a mix of ethnically and gender-differentiated dancers' bodies constituting one single pirouette, and Michael Jackson's morphing of similar bodies into one another in his *Black or White* video clip (John Landis 1991). Sobchack argues that whereas through cut transitions in *All that Jazz* "we are still aware of their discretion and difference …[,] in *Black or White* … these racially and ethnically 'different' singing heads enjoy no discretion: each is never 'itself' but rather a mutable permutation of a single self-similarity [as Jean Baudrillard writes:] 'Division has been replaced by mere propagation'" (ibid.: 142).

The idea that morphing is based on the propagation of inter-referring simulations that deny meaningful categorical or hierarchical differentiations pervades many contemporary films. This can be found in the widespread device of digital replication and multiplication of the same character (e.g., Mr. Smith the virus agent in *The Matrix*) but is also evident in the destabilization of real versus fictional characters or environments in films. Well known cases include Ridley Scott's director's-cut version of *Blade Runner* (1982)—where Deckard, a "blade runner" in charge of tracking down and terminating "replicants," turns out to be a replicant himself.

3.3.1.2. Intertextuality and Split Subjects

Just as many postmodernists consider the search for truth to be unfeasible, so, many reject the modernist notions that an artwork, a grouping of artworks according to authorial or generic categories, or a viewer, are enclosed, discreet, autonomous entities with boundaries and specific internal structures that can be objectively decoded.

Postmodernists redefined text, genre, spectator, and author as "open," inconsistent, and nonessentialist entities. Hence, Michel Foucault asked, how do you decide which texts are subsumed under an author's body of work? Why should a list for the grocery store not be included in the work? Anyway, he asked, who is this "author"? Is it the biological entity it refers to? Is it the structural category con-

structed a posteriori from a group of works carrying the name? If
so, does not the same body of work generate different author categories? Moreover, are we speaking of the same entity across time?
Is a fiction author (to whom authority over the work is ascribed)
similar to a scientific author (where authority is usually denied except
in fictional mythologies of scientists)? (Foucault 1984: 101–102).
This series of questions dismantled the validity or legitimacy of the
modernist category of author. It led Foucault to shift his focus of attention away from questions concerning some elusive essence of an
"author," toward the study of the historically shifting discourses on
what an author is; the ideological or practical interests each discourse
serves; and the consequences of these discourses for people and for
textual studies. A similar procedure was applied by Jacques Derrida
to the structural categories of genre, text, and narrative. He reached
the conclusion that genre and text (the latter designating the enclosed
entities whose grouping constitutes genre) as well as the category narrative, which imposes temporal order on texts, are nothing but fictional constructs and meanings artificially imposed upon an endless
chain of signifiers. He considered these signifiers to potentially emanate indefinite interpretative possibilities (Derrida 1980). This deconstruction of modernist categories had deep consequences for any
claims to objective decoding since if there is no possibility to define
boundaries, there is also no place for talking, as structuralism suggested, about a text's enclosed constitutive units and their "internally"
construed meaning. In fact, all (always arbitrarily posited) units may
in principle be related to any other units, be it from within or from
without a given textual configuration. This also collapsed the modernist divide between deep and manifest meanings, since without the
ability to objectively justify unit groupings, the decision to posit one
group as determining another is arbitrary. As Jameson noted, this
conception delegitimized the Marxist division of a base structure as
determinant of the manifest superstructure, the psychoanalytic distinction between manifest consciousness and its determining underlying unconscious, and the Saussurean linguistic distinction between
manifest speech and the deeper, determining, systemic structure of
language (Jameson 1991).

Concerning the latter, Julia Kristeva and Roland Barthes (in his later writings) dismantled the attempts to ground textual analyses on Saussure-inspired semiology. The struggle to discern objective rules determining textual production was not only considered by them to be futile but was also perceived as an ideological attempt to control cultural production. Postmodernists turned to the dismantling of textual fixtures. They premised that language and other forms of communication are polysemous and multidirectional. Any attempt to fix, stabilize, or systematize the process of signification was in their minds an attempt to control human and textual freedom and creativity. Kristeva's and Barthes's notion of textual and human freedom was based upon a conception of a constantly mutating text and an individual who is: "a divided subject, even a pluralized subject that occupies not a place of enunciation, but permutable, multiple, and mobile places" (Kristeva 1980: 111). Following Mikhail Bakhtin's literary research, particularly his notion that the meaning of a word in a literary text is not fixed but results from its dialogue with various voices and positions within the text, between texts, and in the reader's mind, Kristeva reached the conclusion that it is impossible to apply any deductions made from a presumed language or sign system to manifest textual articulations. Moreover, the whole notion of language as having a priori stable structures was questionable and irrelevant for textual understanding: "The text ... is therefore a productivity, and this means: first, that its relationship to the language in which it is situated is redistributive (destructive-constructive) ... and second, that it is a permutation of texts, an intertextuality: in the space of a given text, several utterances, taken from other texts, intersect and neutralize one another" (ibid.: 36). The early semiological view that texts result from a fixed set of rules internalized in an individual's mind and determining the meaning of the text was exchanged for a conception of the text as intertext: an open set of textual intersections and relations differently realized in each interrelation with a reader or viewer, themselves conceived as having split, shifting identities and entertaining varying positions toward the text. Barthes also changed his mind concerning the valence of his early semiology and began to view the text as "experienced only in an activity of production … its constitutive movement is that of cutting across … [;] it cannot be contained in a hierarchy, even in a simple division of genres" (Barthes 1977: 157).

Postmodern film scholars indeed engendered an approach that can be termed genre-as-process. This approach, heralded by Steve Neale, Adam Knee, and Tag Gallagher, proposed to define genre not according to its recurring elements but rather according to its constantly changing ones. According to Neale, the genre category is mixed to begin with, since genres show mutability and variability. Hence he tried to differentiate genres according to their genre mix (Neale 1995). A more radical approach was offered by Adam Knee who claimed that while there are attempts to contain genres within "[i]ron filings held in position by the magnetic force field of ideology" (Knee 1995: 32), genres by their shifting textual nature evade such static and essentialist impositions. He also dismissed attempts to contain generic evolution in the frame of orderly causal procession by showing that there are so many variables that may cause change (e.g., natural disasters) that it is practically impossible to comprehensibly account for generic change. Finally, Gallagher dismantled attempts to describe an evolution of the western genre by showing that all the signs relegated exclusively to later westerns already appeared in early ones (Gallagher 1995).

This intertextual approach also generated the postmodern type of textual production, perceived as constantly evading categorical typologies and subverting them. This can be somewhat evidenced in films such as Quentin Tarantino's *Pulp Fiction* (1994), a film characterized by the scrambling of temporal order, the mixing of genres, a pastiche of quotes taken from previous films or other cultural forms, and a leveling of light and heavy discourses with an utter disregard for hierarchical distinctions between high and low art. Hence, *Pulp Fiction* starts in the middle, unnoticeably backtracks to the beginning of the story, and reconnects back to where the film began while its protagonists, two hired killers, talk with the same level of affect or seriousness about McDonald's Quarter Pounders, their last bloody murder, and the Bible.

The radical, revolutionary-spirited dismantling of modernist categories used in literary, cinematic, and other cultural research and production, productive in its questioning of attempts at constituting textual meanings as reliable, specific, and objective, also gave vent to discourses that were earlier silenced or repressed. Particularly interesting in this respect is the queer approach and methodology. Hence, "Queer theory shares with feminism an interest in non-straight normative expressions of gender and with lesbian, gay, and bisexual studies a concern with non-straight expressions of sexuality and gender" (Doty 1998: 50). However, what turns queer theory into a postmodern approach is not its legitimizing of nonstraight discourses but rather its going beyond these perspectives in that it focuses upon a generalized notion of transgression concerning any established gender or sexual identity, be it straight, gay, or lesbian. Hence, rather than presuming a fixed or essentialist stable identity, even if this identity is fixed-as-fluid the way postfeminists often characterized femininity, queer theory presumes all sexual and gender identities to be hybrid and in a potential or actual fluid state. In fact, queer theory critiqued the long-held binary opposition of male to female identities that still resonated in the writings of postfeminists. It argued that this binary opposition was designed to exclude varied sexual and social subjects assuming gay, lesbian, bisexual, and transgender identities, since the latter, when viewed from the point of view of the male/female divide, were considered abnormal digressions. Judith Butler's *Gender Trouble* (1990) expanded the (post)feminist position on femininity as diverse, split, shifting, and polysemous, to characterize all sexual identities.[11] She claimed feminism was altogether wrong in its presumption that women or men are groups with clear gender attributes. In her mind, biological sexual differences do not determine gender characteristics or imply a desire for the other sex. While "bodies matter," as she later claimed, gender and sexual desire are seen as variables that may change in different contexts. She proposed to view gender as something both assigned to and assumed by people, as a performance on their part rather than as an inextricably fixed, essential, or inescapably culturally determined identity. As she put it: "There is no gender identity behind the expressions of gender; identity is performatively constituted by the very 'expressions' that are said to be its results" (ibid.: 25). In this respect queer theory seems to be more "postmodern" than the postfeminist and established gay or lesbian approaches whose discourse it helped to legitimize. This is because it emphasizes the constant potential or actual "bending" or "queering" of sexual and gender orientations, rather than being an umbrella term for nonstraight and postfeminist approaches. Moreover, queer theory's fluid gender conception coalesced with the intertextual notion of texts as polysemous, as always "open" to different decoding sensibilities. This led queer theorists of film to herald the spectacular aspect of movies over and above their narrative trajectory, viewing the film's narrative vectorial thrust as being constantly dismantled by, or even irrelevant to the visual pleasures derived by differently gendered spectators from the polysemous and multidirectional nature of the film spectacle. This focus upon spectacle engendered, for example, the growing attention to the spectacular film-star figure described by Richard Dyer as "unstable, never at a point of rest or equilibrium, constantly lurching from one formulation of what being human is to another" (Dyer 1986: 18). The multifaceted and polysemous phenomenon of film stars as complex configurations who operate beyond the confines of a film's narrative trajectory through their various intertextual references easily lends itself to a variety of visual pleasures for a variety of viewers' gender, sexual, and ideological sensibilities. In other words, queer film theory began viewing film spectacles as the "intersection or combination of more than one established 'non-straight' sexuality or gender position in a spectator, a text, or a personality" (Doty 1998: 149).

To sum up, the state desired by neo-Marxists, yet hardly achievable, of a split subject is considered by most postmodernists to be our regular, basic, fluid mental situation. This is complemented by a conception of the text or movie as an intertext, an open, polysemous set of textual intersections and relations differently realized in each interrelation with a split reader or viewer entertaining shifting positions toward the text. Therefore, according to the postmodern premises, the notion of or attempt at imposing narrative causality and closure is a poor and even futile attempt at anchoring a particular trajectory and meaning to the inherently polysemous and evasive textual or movie flow. This impossible narrative imposition is also due, at least according to queer theories of film, to the fact that the major import of movies inheres in their polysemous spectacular aspect. This aspect and the visual pleasure it provides work against and dismantle attempts at imposing narrative ordering. While early postmodernists such as Kristeva and Barthes argued against attempts at the imposition of narratives and closures, suggesting instead narrative openness and decenteredness, in principle and according to their premises as will be discussed below, their argument should have been that such attempts must surely fail in face of their being perceived by mutable viewers and being a priori ineffective given the phenomenon of intertextual polysemy.

It is in these respects that postmodernists consider the progressive causal thrust and narrative closure in movies as futile attempts to engender a single and exclusive meaning. This is not only because films are inherently polysemous, but because as viewers, in our split, fluid, and mutating identity, we generate shifting intertextual relations that "cut across" the given audiovisual film configuration presented before us. It is in this latter sense that postmodernism also implies that the interrelations of movies and viewers engender almost by definition something akin to optional thinking.

3.3.2. Postmodernism and Optional Thinking
—a Failed Alternative

3.3.2.1. Subjective Truisms, Self-contradiction, and Split Attention

Baudrillard's notion of the simulacrum, implying that there is no truth but only subjective truisms, is ineffective for viable optional thinking. Its reduction and leveling of all articulations into inter-referring simulations, based upon the unwarranted notion that the simulacrum has no origin, and that this "origin" is but an empty concept aimed at installing false hierarchies among even simulations, is self-defeating. It implies loopy thinking in that it conceptualizes perception and cognition as being caught in a mental prison, entertaining recursively optional simulations that are all equally invalid. This self-defeating loopy perception and cognition can be evidenced in Baudrillard's own position. In his writings, Baudrillard tries to articulate a critique of society's devices to instill a sense of hierarchy and meaning so as to salvage the different institutions' fake legitimacy, allowing these to maintain their privileges (e.g., the political system, psychology, ethnography, and archeology) (Baudrillard 1995a). Elsewhere he describes the situation as "a masquerade of information: branded faces delivered over to the prostitution of the image, the image of an unintelligible distress" (1995b: 40). However, such criticism is unwarranted because, according to Baudrillard's own premises, his notions of privilege or distress cannot be but simulacra and therefore cannot claim by definition to offer a more proper or valid description of phenomena.[12] David Cronenberg's film *eXistenZ* (1999), mentioned on p. 16, where a game designer creates a virtual-reality game that taps into the players' body and mind but ultimately leaves them (and us) with the idea that the "reality" from which the film started may have been just another option within the game, is an emblematic example of the loopy thinking that Baudrillard's notion of the simulacrum encourages (I will return again to this movie on p. 102).

Just as the notion of the simulacrum implies that there is no truth but only "subjective truisms," defining texts to begin with as multidirectional, shifting, and polysemous on all levels renders any attribution of this or that interrelation between texts or textual segments arbitrary. This is perhaps why Barthes described the intertextual process in terms of a nonobliging game (1977: 155–165), while other postmodernists gave up altogether upon notions of textual truth-search and objectivity.

It should be noted, however, that the widespread presumption of polysemy, particularly when it is considered to be determined by the arbitrary nature of signifiers (a notion elaborated upon by Derrida but shared by many postmodernists), is not only unwarranted but incomprehensible. Actually, it is the other way around. It is only because we can cognitively and perceptually manipulate signifiers in order to forge conventions that will render nonarbitrary articulations that are comprehensible and communicative, that sign systems are used and serve us so well. Likewise, while our mental faculties allow the conception of change, this change can be meaningfully conceived or registered only in respect of constants and restrictions, whether conceptual, psychological, or material. There are no comprehensible changes without constants just as there are no comprehensible constants without change. In the postmodern episteme, as described by Baudrillard, "Division has been replaced by mere propagation," ending up in the propagation of inter-referring simulations that deny meaningful categorical or hierarchical differentiation. Moreover, the postmodern episteme seems to forego the notion that film constructs are indeed in the film text rather than subjectively imposed, and that these are usually *reconstructed* successfully by the minds of coherence-seeking spectators. Finally, in their presumption of an inherently mutable and split subject, postmodernists fail to notice the deep engagement resulting from the interaction between narrative films' intended, textually embedded narrative and the cognitively and emotionally active spectators, deeply engaged by the films' modes of narrative delivery in satisfyingly reconstructing the narrative in their minds.

While postmodern approaches to genre, author, narrative, and text have proved fruitful in deconstructing modernist structuralist or semiological certainties, their perception of a boundless, decentered textual universe in itself generates a theoretical and practical labyrinth. This labyrinth emerges when the impulse that led to deconstruction attempts to reconstruct the concepts it had earlier dismantled. For example, the postmodern attempts at genre reconstruction made by Neale (1995) are paradoxical. This is simply because the attempt to differentiate genres according to their genre mix, while claiming that genres are always-already mixed, logically demands that they presume unmixed portions that are then mixed. But since according to their premises there are not such unmixed portions to begin with, how can someone decide *what* is mixed?

The same paradox resurfaces in the postmodern, unwarranted attempt at labeling narrative structures as futile impositions of order upon an inherently polysemous text-as-intertext, including their consequent suggestions to reconstruct the concept of narrative as open and decentered, or the attendant queer theory predilection of the "spectacular," nonnarrative aspect of films over their presumably ineffectual narrative constructs. This is because the attempt to define textual narrative trajectories as open ended or decentered logically demands that there be trajectories that are then made open or decentered. But according to the postmodern intertextual definition of texts, how can something that is defined to begin with as decentered and open be decentred or opened? Likewise, the widespread, postmodern critique of the "imposition" of a narrative structure on polysemous texts, which, as queer theorists suggest, is being constantly dismantled by viewers' subjective and shifting, differing sensibilities, and resisted by the films' intertextual polysemy, is unwarranted as a constant, as is their own predilection for the "speculative," intertextual, nonnarrative aspect of films.

Queer theorists have no good reason to divide films as intertexts into narrative and/or "spectacular" arrangements. According to their own premises, spectacular organizations result solely from different viewers' bendable predilections, to which films presumably "bend." In this latter respect, the "text" as intertext is inconsequential to its decoding since it seems to lend itself in principle to any subjective decoding. Moreover, even if we discard queer theory's lack of rationale for its decoding of, and distinction between the narrative trajectory in films and their "spectacular" aspect,[13] accepting for a moment its suggestion that narrative trajectories are mere excuses or clothes hangers for the deployment of a spectacular polysemy, this does not imply viewers' optional thinking. While the spectacular layer of movies may "open" them to a variety of nonnarrative visual pleasures or subjective associations for viewers with different sensibilities, the evident fact that for some viewers, sometimes, polysemous portions of the spectacle may trigger localized, subjective associations or gender-specific visual pleasures does not imply a viable trajectory for optional thinking in terms of causes and consequences that are meaningfully optional to other such trajectories. In fact, if viewers manage to construe a trajectory out of a spectacular portion where narrative is disjointed, this must surely come on account of the attention required to construe the narrative, causal chaining of these spectacular portions. In a way, a viewer "poaching" disjointed segments in order to construe a subjectively preferred interrelation dismantles a narrative film's inherent cohering structures and has little to do with viable optional thinking.

The postmodern perception of texts as constantly shifting configurations of variables is self-contradictory in that it cannot remove determining invariables, simply because one cannot specify a difference unless there is a constant against which to measure it.[14] This is also why postmodernist tenets offer a failed alternative to viable optional thinking, since in order to entertain an alternative there has to be something comprehensible in relation to which another (preferably) comprehensible thing may be posed as its alternative. However, if all things are variously comprehended, nothing can be posed as an alternative, for any such "alternative" can also be comprehended as that to which it is arbitrarily posed as different. Thus, postmodernism, in its suggestion to totally exchange constancy by a (self-contradictory) notion of total inconstancy, renders incomprehensible both the concept of optional thinking and that of closed mindedness.

Just as postmodern decoding practices fail to abide by their premises, comprehensible films oriented by postmodern premises are comprehensible because of their textually embedded and decodable orderings. Thus, postmodern films such as Tarantino's *Pulp Fiction*, which offers an apparently open-ended and decentered narrative, is comprehensible not because of its inherent openness or decenteredness (e.g., Brunette and Wills 1989) but because of its offering a temporal scrambling that, while not altogether adding up to a fully comprehensible reordering, does offer a more or less comprehensible closed and centered narrative. Moreover, *Pulp Fiction*'s temporal scrambling is articulated through a rather traditional use of strategies of suspense, surprise, character "focalization," and cataphora–anaphora interplay.

In fact, I contend that *Pulp Fiction*'s scrambled temporality would have turned, for most viewers, into an incomprehensible, confusing, distracting, and disengaging audiovisual configuration if it lacked embedded or decodable cohering strategies and an overall notion of a comprehensible narrative trajectory leading to closure. This is so because while some viewers, as postmodernists suggest, might decipher vague intertextual relations among some of the films' features, viewers facing such decentered intertextual "openness" are required to simultaneously consider an array of shifting polysemies opening up various interrelations. This engenders split attention, a situation that few, if any real people are capable of dealing with in a cognitively effective manner (Chandler and Sweller 1991). Thus, beyond the logical fallacy implied in postmodernism, postmodern film narrative theorists seem to overlook the embedded consequences of a split attention engendered by decentered and "open" audiovisual configurations. Wrongly presuming that splitting the viewer's attention caters to the characterizing and desired form of perception in our age, postmodernists entertain a confounded belief that "opening" the text to whatever viewers want to invest in it is feasible, or that viewers can meaningfully invest in such a text. This notion is confounded because closure and cohering strategies are the *sine qua non* components that enable the cognitively rewarding engagement of spectators with films. In a sense, the whole notion of narration is meaningless if the viewer's aspiration for coherence and closure is frustrated to begin with. It is only because texts offer you a notion that they are going somewhere that you are willing to follow. The tenets of postmodernism, or films that try to strictly abide by these, imply at best shallow viewer distraction rather than cognitive attention or viable optional thinking. The widespread practice of flicking channels in television or roaming the internet instantiates this distractive viewing. In other words, postmodernists wrongly presume a subject capable of being attentive while splitting his/her attention (Ben Shaul 2008: 18–23). This can be evidenced in Mike Figgis's film *Timecode*.

In this film, four simultaneously evolving occurrences are presented on a screen split into four parts. However, whether it is the same occurrence shot from different positions, or different occurrences, it is impossible for the spectator's split attention to follow what is going on simultaneously in all screens.[15] The only reason viewers can somehow follow Figgis's film is because he manages to draw attention away from the disturbing parallel occurrences through different strategies that accentuate one frame over the others, such as his use of voice enhancement coming from one of the screens, or the reduction to minimal, recurring, and uninteresting movement and action in the unemphasized screens; by using a sporadically appearing earthquake that affects all the events on the four screens; or, toward the end, by the use of a melodramatic shootout of a betrayed lover that correlates and clarifies in a simple manner the interrelation between the four screens. There is, however, one interesting use of the split screen, in which we see on one screen the betrayed lover eavesdropping on her girlfriend through a microphone she planted in the latter's bag, while on another screen we see the girlfriend as she makes love to a man the betrayed lover does not know. Then, within her screen we see the betrayed lover get out of the car she is in, while the man her girlfriend was with is seen in the other screen leaving a building, and they bump into each other in their respective screens without knowing each other (this is the man she eventually shoots by the end of the film) so that we see simultaneously the same occurrence from different angles. This scene is interesting because it is a cohering rather than a distracting use of the split screen, in that it makes literal through the form the implications of betrayal.[16] Excluding this coherent use of the split screen (which still occurs in only two of the four screens), it seems that it mostly manages to engage attention in those aspects that contradict its intended formation. The response encouraged in viewers by this film is distraction coupled with partial engagement.

Interestingly, some postmodernists, in a dialectic leap, have turned to consider how their axiomatic notion of constant mutability may be structured so as to render it comprehensible, thus trying to bridge the gap between narrative-cohering "end products" and their oxymoronic notion of an open, process-oriented, closure-less narrative. Such is Manovich's suggested "data-base narrative" approach (Manovich 2001), picked up by Kinder who defines it as

> those narratives, whether in novels, films or games, whose structure exposes the dual processes of selection and combination that lie at the heart of all stories and that are crucial to language: the selection of particular data (characters, images, sounds, events) from a series of databases or paradigms, which are then combined to generate specific tales. (Kinder 2002: 127)

Kinder's approach suggests a foregrounding of a synchronic structure within which different diachronic narrative trajectories are played out. As such, this emergent form may evoke optional thinking (see chapter 4). However, Kinder's postmodern comprehension of narrative gears her toward highlighting the arbitrariness entailed in this emergent form, whereby she relegates closure to structure and "openness" to the narrative tracks. This is implied in her statement that such movies "reveal the arbitrariness of the particular choices made, and the possibility of making other combinations, which would create alternative stories (ibid.). While Kinder's postmodernism considers arbitrariness a virtue, it is a stumbling block for knowledge acquisition and optional thinking. In fact, arbitrariness, which Kinder finds "at the heart" of narratives, dismantles the probabilistic causality characterizing narratives. This encourages a game-like, decontextualized form of optional thinking (Ben Shaul 2008; Simons 2007). It may also encourage a fear of invalidity out of uncertainty as to what is meant by the "open" narrative trajectories, thus heightening the need to alleviate uncertainty with a gratifying resolution or closure.[17] However, the attainment of such closure is impeded, given the unresolved "open" narrations. Movies abiding by this arbitrary kind of "data-base narratives" reciprocate this impasse encouraged in the viewer by imposing the foregrounded structure as arbitrary closure. This encourages viewers to readily accept the labyrinthine "closure on non-closure," along with an attendant loopy mentality.

Consider again David Cronenberg's *eXistenZ*, a science-fiction psychological thriller about characters caught in a virtual game. The film starts with an event where a virtual-reality game designed by Allegra Geller (Jennifer Jason Leigh), "the greatest game designer in the world," is being played by several participants with an organic game console known as a "game pod" that is inserted into the player's spine through a "bio-port." In the midst of the game an intruder enters the room and shoots Allegra, wounding her. She is carried away by a security guard named Ted Pikul (Jude Law) and they both end up in a shabby motel room. There, Allegra convinces the reluctant Ted to insert a bio-port into his body so that they can both hook up to "eXistenZ" to test the game, which she fears has been damaged. They head to a gas station run by a man named Gas (Willem Dafoe) to get it installed and Gas, after installing a damaged bio-port into Ted, tries to kill Allegra for the bounty on her head, but Ted shoots him first. Once Allegra and Ted are trans-

ported into the game, whose rules and goals are unknown to Ted
and unpredictable to Allegra due to the way she designed the game,
they are given clues by different lifelike characters that lead them
from one weird encounter to the next, amidst an ambiance of vague
conspiracies apparently stemming from a competition between two
virtual game companies (Antenna Research and Cortical Systemat-
ics) and between these and a group of underground "realist" fight-
ers that try to prevent the "deforming" of reality. This "deforming" theme runs throughout the game, constantly confounding the
virtual with the real as in the inadvertent appearance of a weird
double-headed lizard in what appears to be the reality portion of
the film; in the encounters of Ted and Allegra within the game with
a virtual, lifelike character that suddenly enters into a computer
bug loop; in Ted's "pausing" the game in order to get back to the
real world, only to find out he is unable to distinguish reality from
illusion; or in Ted's realization within the game that some of his
actions are not his own but imposed by the game. This occurs, for
example, when Ted and Allegra meet D'Arcy Nader (Robert A. Sil-
verman), a video-game shop owner: Ted suddenly speaks rudely to
him, but later learns from Allegra that it was Ted's game character
that made him speak like that. This overpowering by the game of
the real Ted recurs when Ted develops a sudden urge to eat a dis-
gusting dish consisting of cooked mutant animals, and in the scene
that concludes the game, where Ted turns against Allegra, revealing
to her that he is actually a "realist" sent to kill her. Upon hearing
this Allegra kills Ted by detonating his bio-port by remote control.
This confounding of the real with the virtual continues after Ted is
killed, when he and Allegra are seen returning to the room where
the film started, being congratulated by the other game participants
for winning the game. However, upon their return they learn that
the whole story from the beginning of the movie, including the
preparations for the game before they began playing it, was actually
part of another virtual reality game called "tranCendenZ," played
by the same players we saw at the beginning of the movie but who
turn out to have been characters of "tranCendenZ." At this point it
becomes unclear whether there was a real site to the movie to begin

with and they are lost in a maze, or whether this is a forward step into a second (or third) game that virtually simulates the real first scene. This confounding is enhanced once Ted and Allegra get into another shootout and game-like events within the real/unreal site. The movie ends with Ted's unanswered question to one of the other players concerning whether they are still within a game.

As can be seen, the characters initially think that the movie's convoluted and arbitrary narrative is taking place within a virtual computer game whose rules and goals they cannot understand. They ultimately win the game by happenstance. However, the arbitrary and convoluted narrative is not clarified when the game "ends," as the characters apparently enter the next game, or an upper level of the same game, whose rules, while new, are as convoluted and arbitrary as those of the preceding game, implying in a sense that further games could be played ad infinitum, each with its own peculiar variation. In this sense, the movie suggests there is no end to the ongoing chaining of games since each ending is "really" the opening of a new game version. This potentially endless "data-base" of game narratives ("eXistenZ," then "tranCendenZ," and then, in principle, another variation) is played out within the confines of the question of whether the characters are in reality or in virtual reality, a binary set that constitutes the movie's structure. This type of "data-base narrative," characterized by tightly contained game variations, that while implying an endless chain are in fact recursive or cyclical variations upon the same binary question, present a Sisyphus-like loopy mentality. I suggest that this mentality is also gradually encouraged in viewers of this movie. Thus, as the movie progresses, Ted tries to get out of the game due to his failure to decipher the rules of the virtual game he is in, only to find out he is unsure of whether the reality he returns to after pausing the game is real. Ted's initial fear of invalid assumptions concerning the rules of the game gradually intensifies once he realizes that initial confidence about what is real and what virtual may also be invalid. This fear of invalidity is also gradually encouraged in viewers, who are not given any advantage over Ted concerning knowledge of the rules of the game, or of what constitutes the real as opposed to the virtual in the movie. This fear of invalidity heightens the need to alleviate it with a gratifying resolution or closure that would resolve the issue.[18] However, the attainment of closure is impeded by the potentially endless game variations implied when the protagonists at the end of the game "eXistenZ" appear to begin the new game "tranCendenZ", which may also be the encompassing game within which "eXistenZ" is embedded. At this point, the viewer's impasse intensifies given the sense of recurrence of virtual game variations, an impasse reciprocated by the movie's imposition of the constant, underlying, binary question of whether we are in the real or the virtual world, as arbitrary structural closure to what in principle could go on indefinitely. I suggest that the movie's closure upon nonclosure readily accepted by the viewers encourages a loopy mentality in them.

This mentality characterizes an array of contemporary films. These include other real/virtual "mobius strip" films such as David Fincher's *Fight Club* (1999) David Lynch's oxymoronic films *Lost Highway* (1997) and *Mullholland Drive* (2001) Spike Jonze/Charlie Kaufman's shifting perspective films *Being John Malkovich* (1999) and *Adaptation* (2002) Christopher Nolan's *Memento* (2000) and his recent film *Inception* (2010). The recurrence of such films has been taken to characterize contemporary cinema by different scholars, who describe them as "modular" (Cameron 2008), "atemporal" (McGowan 2011), "puzzle" (Buckland 2009), "complex" (Simons 2008), or "mind-game" films (Elsaesser 2009). The narrative complexity characterizing such films has been meaningfully related by these scholars to pressures brought upon the conventional, linear narrative movie structure by the nonlinear hypercontext of much digital and interactive production. Likewise, some scholars, in a manner akin to mine, have found the formal and thematic characteristics of these films to be indexes of the anxieties of disorientation felt by subjects in an incomprehensible globalization process and its attendant postmodern episteme. However, contrary to my position on the films discussed above, these scholars often find in them what Elsaesser has termed "productive pathologies" that apparently offer ways out of the postmodern maze. Elsaesser, for example, finds the amnesiac, reversed story and guiding formal and thematically subjective point of view of Leonard Shelby (Guy Pearce) in Nolan's *Memento* as "foregrounding the idea of 'programming,' as opposed to remembering .... Leonard represents ... the new multitasking personality (dissociative, reactive: not rapid reaction but random reaction force) ... its mental instability and volatility potentially more efficient" (ibid.: 29). Also Simons (2007), in discussing *Memento*, finds in the protagonist's disturbing retroactive tracing of the loose causal chain that led to his amnesia and in the attendant exchange of causes for results a cinematic reference to contemporary chaos or complexity theories. This is because the loosening and reversal of the causal chain in the movie points to, or raises in viewers the presumptions of chaos or complexity theory about an array of causal chains that are hard or impossible to configure, and which lead to an array of forking possibilities from any given moment.

Elsaesser's rather romantic adoption of the advantages of pathologies for creativity may offer valuable insights into the mind, and may even encourage random, localized yet vague optional thinking in viewers of *Memento*. However, the disjointed dynamic of the backtracking narrative, figuring and formally replicating the mentality of its mentally unstable protagonist, rather ends up encouraging in viewers an intense attention, heightening their need for closure, along with an intense fear of invalidity due to the random and dissociative narrative. While this process is intriguing, in that it evidences the cognitive ability of viewers to manage to nevertheless follow and figure out the narrative,[19] it nevertheless ends up encouraging loopy thinking both in the required and repetitive back-and-forth puzzle-solving activity, and in the latter's short-circuiting at the end by a loop that returns the viewer to the film's opening shot. Likewise, while Simons's adopted chaos theory may offer valuable insights into reality, it is very hard to understand how the intense back-and-forth process of the film's plot reconstruction in the viewers' mind might encourage optional thinking. This is particularly so given the viewer's primary and usually successful goal of causal reconstruction of the admittedly loose causality of this movie. In fact, and irrespective of *Memento*, while the philosophical or scientific implication of chaos theory is an intriguing narrative *idea* implying endless forking story possibilities, attempts to actually devise such narratives are impossible, nor will a viewer be able to comprehensibly trace such process. Moreover, these attempts are unnecessary since this idea can be fruitfully evoked and explored by the suggestion of its implications through two or three optional yet causal narrative trajectories.

Finally, while it is perfectly reasonable to discuss the trend to produce movies that evidence complex narrative structures, these are often lumped together and their crucial differences disregarded: there is no differentiation between movies presenting and encouraging loopy, split, or optional thinking. As will be discussed in the following chapter, not all movies foregrounding their narrative architecture as part and parcel of their narrative progression render split or loopy thinking. As I will show, some such movies present and may encourage a powerful process of optional thinking (e.g., *Sliding Doors*). This is precisely because in these movies, the optional narratives are not "open" but lead in turn to a different gratifying closure and resolution. Therefore, they do not "impose" structural closure upon a cyclical recurrence of "open" alternatives, but rather indicate that each option directs to a different causal trajectory and resolving closure and does not revolve around an irresolvable set of alternatives.

While postmodern theories are marred by the misleading notion of intertextuality as an open and endless process along with the attendant sense of arbitrariness, some postmodernists have suggested productive models that may help discern movies encouraging optional thinking once their notions of open intertextuality are withheld. Hence, Ziva Ben-Porath has suggested evaluating the relations between texts according to the degree of dependence a derived text has on its originating text, in terms of the degree of freedom or disorder that the intertextual relation allows readers or viewers. This led her to place different types of texts along a continuum stretching from highly dependent texts, allowing little freedom in the realization of intertextual relations as in parodies, to highly independent ones such as texts based on metaphorical allusions to others. Ben-Porath instantiates the difference in degree of depen-

dency in types of intertextual relations, by considering the difference between the sentences: "Diana mews like a cat" and "Diana
resembles a cat." While in the former sentence "Diana" is highly dependent upon "cat" and the reader's freedom in the materialization
of the intertextual relation is low since only "mewing" is shared by
both texts, in the latter sentence the reader has more freedom since
Diana can resemble the cat in different ways (Ben-Porath 1983).
Ben-Porath's favorable notion of intertextual "freedom" falls into
the postmodern trap discussed above, in that from a certain point
in her "continuum" sporadic references from text to text become
arbitrary. However, once this meaningless notion of "freedom" is
discarded, the discussion of parodies, satires, and particularly what
she calls "pseudo-metonymical allusions" or texts that critically revise their originating text may engender viable optional thinking.
This occurs, however, precisely because such texts are constrained
in a compelling way by the originating text as will be discussed and
instantiated in the following chapter.

Another useful model for optional thinking which originally
stemmed from postmodern thought was suggested by Alexander
Doty. His queer theory is productive when arguing that movies
may offer viable, different, simultaneously present perspectives and
comprehensions that extend throughout a film's cohering narrative
trajectory and single closure (see Doty 2000). Doty attributes these
simultaneous different perspectives to viewers pertaining to different "interpretive communities" or with different sexual orientations,
problematically implying that this is possible due to movies' inherent
"open" polysemy. However, once we remove this implied "openness"
whereby any viewer may read anything into the open polysemy, the
notion of a semantic conflation that clearly contains its divergent
meanings may be in principle extended to articulate through a single
narrative trajectory differing yet simultaneous and cohering optional
perspectives. I will discuss the feasibility of such options in the concluding chapter.

As this chapter's discussion of formalism, neo-Marxism, and postmodernism suggests, not providing narrative coherence and closure
to movies or the dismantling of suspense or surprise constructs do not

encourage viable optional thinking. The detached attention to formal patterning on account of narrative (formalism), the deconstruction of movie narratives (neo-Marxism), and the devise of "open," arbitrary, or causally faulty narratives (postmodernism) usually offer failed alternatives in terms of provoking optional thinking. This is because approaches such as these undermine the possibility of couching narrative movies' probabilistic causality within a coherent narrative leading to closure, along with the highly engaging use of surprise and suspense structures which are the *sine qua non* of movies. Disruptions of these conditions, while necessarily teasing viewers toward narrative construction, renders split attention, and enhances the viewer's sense of arbitrariness, loopy thinking, lack of comprehension, distraction, confusion, vagueness, frustration, or boredom.

Notes

1. It is not necessarily the case as Tynjanov holds, that the structure of story as chronological ordering of events into a beginning, middle and end is "natural," or that it stems from a "standard real-life" perception.

2. Not paying attention to the revolutionary thematic thrust underlying these films' formal experimentation, or to the propagandistic rationale underlying their simple story structure, leads to aimless mental rumination rather than to optional thinking. Conversely, paying attention to these ideological form-content configurations, as intended by the filmmakers, results in the comprehension that their aim was to block rather than evoke optional thinking. This is particularly evident in Eisenstein's notion of a montage of conflicts as a movie blow ("*Kino-Fist*"); in his notion of pathos; and in the application of these strategies to portray a revolutionary historical event. Indeed, Eisenstein strived to control the viewer's physiological, emotional, and intellectual processes and direct these toward an exclusive, Marxist perception of the world (Eisenstein 1949).

3. See also my discussion of formalism in its relation to realist and Marxist approaches to film (Ben Shaul 2008).

4. Reflexivity is particularly popular in neo-Marxist film theories. We will take up this neo-Marxist presupposition in the following section.

5. Such a split and the predilection of form over content is evident in Lev Manovich's misguided comprehension of *The Man with a Movie Camera*. Manovich does offer an interesting comparison between Vertov's project and his own "data-base narrative" model, in that Vertov's film shows the process of tracing trajectories (comparable to algorithms according to Manovich) across a data base of the documentary images Vertov has gathered. However, Manovich

bases his comparison upon a misguided comprehension of the film's narrative, probably due to his attention being split even while analysing it. Thus, he conceives Vertov's film in terms of a narrative lacking closure (2001: 227–228). This is evidenced in his understanding of what he terms Vertov's major achievement in "how to merge database and narrative into a new form," whereby narrative is described as the open-ended narrative of the discovery of cinematic effects, "an untamed, and apparently endless, unwinding of techniques" (ibid.: 242–243). He is thus oblivious to Vertov's major ideological and aesthetic goal of aspiring to a communist decoding of the total social process, through cohering closure strategies. These are found in the film's overlapping of a film-screening process from beginning to end with a full morning-to-evening cycle of a city's life, and a spatial expansion explicating the interrelations of the various forces and means of production in Soviet society at the time. Manovich's convenient underestimation of Vertov's cinematic implementation of his aspiration for a total comprehension of the mode of production, cardinal to Vertov's communist ideology, allows him to anachronistically place Vertov on the side of a formalist-cum-postmodern closureless episteme.

6. An interesting example in film is Michael Snow's *Wavelength* (1967), brilliantly commented upon by Annette Michelson (1979). In this film, consisting of a lengthy, forty-minute zoom that crosses an empty loft and ends on a meaningless, still photograph appended to the opposite wall, the support lent by a film's visual flow to the expectancy otherwise engendered by the narrative is laid bare. The film manages to evoke in trained and very patient viewers thoughts about how their perception and cognition are directed by audiovisual strategies. This does not mean, as Michelson's analysis implies, that the film has no content or narrative, but rather that its content and (boring) narrative revolve precisely upon the laying bare of the support lent by a film's visual flow to the expectancy otherwise engendered by the narrative.

7. This idea that forms in and of themselves carry an ideological import can be traced back to the Marxist-Soviet revolutionary, avant-garde film of the 1920s, particularly to Eisenstein's notion of formal conflict as embedding the idea of dialectic materialism. Thus, for Eisenstein, the formal clash of shots corresponded to the dialectic clash of thesis and antithesis whose effect upon the viewer corresponded to the synthesis in the dialectic triad. He maintained that viewer manipulation towards a revolutionary mentality was more effective through a montage of conflicts since it suggested that the social reality depicted in the film (and by association, social reality at large) was manmade rather than god given. However, while the dynamism of subject matter may arguably be more sensually, affectively, and cognitively sweeping through use of montage of conflict strategies rather than (fast-paced) continuity editing, it does not follow that formal articulations embed ideological viewpoints irrespective of the contents articulated. Thus, Eisensteinian montage strategies are often used in film or television commercials for selling products or ideas that are antithetical to a Marxist revolutionary mentality.

8. For a critique of the uselessness of such an encompassing conception of ideology, as well as a critique of the far-fetched Althusserian film scholars' pre-

sumptions about viewers' identification with the camera's point of view, of the unwarranted notion that viewers take the reality portrayed by the fiction film to be real, or of the weird and counterfactual idea that viewers are led to believe by centering strategies that they "control" or "originate" the movie, see N. Carroll (1988).

9. A good example is *Austin Powers, the Spy Who Shagged Me* (Jay Roach 1999) which offers a nostalgic return to an idealized, explicitly fake image of the 1960s through intertextual references to James Bond films.

10. There are different versions of postmodern theory, including theories that have a different relationship to neo-Marxist theory than the one held by Jameson. This is particularly the case with postcolonial theory (a relative of postmodernism) that presumes that the notion of the split or "hybrid" subject evidences a revolutionary mentality as predicted by neo-Marxists, in that a hybrid mentality subversively destabilizes and dismantles the elite's attempts at consolidating their ideologies (e.g., Bhaba 1990: 291–322). It is my contention, however, that rather than promoting subversion, Bhaba's stance partakes in the postmodern leveling, neutralization, and ultimate subduing of any potential subversion to the interests of the elites (see more in Ben Shaul 2008: 26). Baudrillard also shows explicit affinity to neo-Marxism in his critique of the simulacrum by a vague appeal to "Capital" as the evil force masked by the episteme of the simulacrum and impervious to it (Baudrillard 1995a). However, as will be discussed, Baudrillard's critique is self-effacing, rendering incomprehensible his notion of "Capital" as something beyond simulation.

11. Butler's queer theory argued that not only deconstructive feminism (e.g., Mulvey 1985: 303–314), in its exchange of biological essentialism with a binary cultural determinism, but also the postfeminists' return to the body as grounds for grouping women, ultimately led to a dead end (e.g., Doan 1982: 74–78; Irigaray 1985).

12. As I have argued elsewhere, Baudrillard's self-effacing, confused critique, negating a process he cannot conceptually escape, is itself a symptom of very real sociopolitical configurations of power in the present situation of globalization, a process his detached concept of the simulacrum helps to efface (Ben Shaul 2008).

13. This distinction was fruitfully exploited by Laura Mulvey in her claim that movies, mapping women onto the passive, to-be-looked-at, spectacular aspect of movies and men into directing the activity-based narrative trajectory, inculcate a patriarchal ideology in viewers. While this is somewhat questionable, it is theoretically feasible given her underlying structuralist tenets (Mulvey 1985).

14. Actually, the postmodern premises of textual boundlessness and decentralization are themselves unjustified invariables.

15. Jameson, in discussing Nam June Paik's video installations, refers to how these exemplify the postmodern "schizophrenic" episteme, in that they frustrate any attempt by visitors to comprehend the whole picture, given the simultaneous details in each of the scattered screens (1991: 39).

16. This is evidence that split screens, as a peculiar formal strategy enhanced by the digital revolution, in themselves do not need to engender split attention.

17. See an explanation of the cognitive psychological dynamic propelling such a mental state in section 2.1. of this book.

18. This impasse is what probably led the producers of Ridley Scott's *Blade Runner* (1982), a movie that also revolves around the question of whether reality can be distinguished from virtual reality, to offer a different cut of the movie than the one Scott originally intended. Thus, while in the director's cut version Deckard (Harrison Ford), a "blade runner" in charge of tracking down and terminating "replicants," turns out to be a replicant himself, thus presenting loopy thinking, in the studio cut version Deckard remains human throughout. Interestingly, in 2007, Warner Bros. released a digitally remastered final cut by Scott.

19. I will return to this capacity later on when discussing some implied cognitivist presumptions about such a capacity in movie viewers.

4

Optional Thinking in Movies

In this chapter I suggest critically reconsidering the cognitive-psychological approach to movies. As already argued in chapter 2, leading cognitive-psychological studies, while identifying the major components that make movies popular, fail to deal with how such movies' specific cognitive affects bias the cognitive process of knowledge construction toward closed mindedness and optional thinking deficiency. In what follows I will argue that film cognitivists inadvertently presume that optional-thinking deficiency is by necessity built into the components that make movies popular and that this is a small price to pay for the various gratifications on offer. I will then suggest that this inadvertent presumption is groundless, and that the components in movies that engender these affects (i.e., narrative audiovisual flow, suspense, surprise, empathy for characters, and the cataphora–anaphora interplay) can also be productively manipulated in order to encourage optional thinking, without such films losing the affective appeal of these components. I will instantiate the latter claim by a detailed analysis of movies that encourage optional thinking.

4.1. Revisiting the Cognitive-Psychological Approach to Movies

My suggestion in chapter 2, that most movies encourage a heightened need for closure which is used to undermine the viewers' optional-thinking capabilities, runs counter to a leading premise of dominant cognitive-psychological approaches to movies, namely, that such movies offer favorable cognitive pleasures to a cognitively active, questioning, or hypothesizing viewer. While the cognitive-psychological approach is the most akin to the constructivist process of knowledge construction guiding this study, and while it has offered the most plausible explanation and description of the narrative structure and strategies of movies, it has so far failed to seriously consider how movies reduce cognitive activity and block optional thinking in viewers. This stems from either ignoring their cognitive affects (e.g., Bordwell), from unnecessarily lauding the pleasures of simplicity (e.g., Carroll), or from heralding the emotional pleasures afforded by these films' cognitive affects on account of their cognitive reductionism and their attendant blocking of optional thinking (e.g., Tan).

According to Bordwell, films, particularly popular narrative films, entertain because they play with the viewers' hypothesizing faculties with digressions or by offering misleading clues. Viewers enjoy movies because they are led to actively hypothesize or raise options as to the probable answers to questions posed.

> In experiencing art [and popular film], instead of focusing on the pragmatic results of perception, we turn our attention to the very process itself. What is non-conscious in everyday mental life becomes consciously attended to. Our schemata get shaped, stretched and transgressed; delay in hypothesis-confirmation can be prolonged for its own sake. (Bordwell 1985: 32)

While this Kantian reflexive view of aesthetic pleasure may explain how optional cognitive processes triggered by films may be pleasurable, Bordwell's admitted disregard for how cognitive processes trigger affect (ibid.: 39) leads him to overlook the salient ways by which most such films constrain and narrow these processes.

Admittedly, Bordwell's analysis of Hitchcock's *Rear Window* (1954), in detecting the various hypotheses opened up in the narrative, does suggest how the movie *might* evoke optional thinking in the viewer. This is mostly due to knowledge gaps between spectator and protagonist and in what Bordwell calls the "narration." Thus, when Jeff (James Stewart), the protagonist, falls asleep, only the viewers, misled by the "narration," see Thorwald (Raymond Burr), whom Jeff suspects has murdered his wife, leaving the apartment accompanied by a woman who may be his wife. Options are also reinforced through their replication in brief vignettes showing minor characters "thematically mirroring" the feasibility of raised optional hypotheses. This occurs, for example, when "Miss Lonely-Hearts" (Judith Evelyn), one of Jeff's neighbors, is distantly seen by Jeff and his girlfriend Lisa (Grace Kelly) being humiliated by her presumed lover. This vignette reinforces by proxy both the counter-hypothesis just raised by Doyle (Wendell Corey), Jeff's detective friend, whereby Thorwald did not kill his wife but rather she left him after a quarrel, and an optional result to Jeff and Lisa's rocky relationship. Finally, options seem viable when followed up, as when Doyle reports to Jeff that the trunk which Jeff presumed carried the murdered body contained only clothes and was presumably picked up by Thorwald's wife.

While *Rear Window* may be taken as indicative of how movies may engender viable optional thinking, Bordwell's disregard of the deliberate extreme vagueness of all options pertaining to the presumed murder (including the one held by Jeff), coupled with intermittent distressing events (e.g., a scream and a murdered dog) that trigger suspense structures, renders questionable whether viewers meaningfully partake reflexively and consciously in the optional hypothesizing process exhibited before them by the characters. I would rather suggest that *Rear Window* exhibits a vague form of optional thinking in the characters but does not elicit viable optional thinking in viewers. This is due, among other reasons, to the movie's strategy of quick, mutual deconstruction of the vaguely and poorly structured alternatives (explicitly argued by Doyle's claim that neither he nor Jeff can know much, based upon the limited evidence at hand). This lack of clarity goes on until only one alternative remains and the fact that Thorwald is the murderer becomes clear and exclusive. Thus, neither the viewer nor the characters, throughout most of the movie, have much to go on in respect to the alternative suggested hypotheses. For viewers, the highly hypothetical and mostly intuitive options entertained by the characters, concerning Thorwald's behavior, leave the viewers with no clue about what is going on in Thorwald's apartment. This situation, along with intermittent aversive surprises and suspense structures, gears viewers toward an unsettling "wait and see" expectancy up until the short (yet highly suspenseful) climax and resolution of the movie.

Notwithstanding *Rear Window*'s intimation of some plot construction strategies that may engender viable optional thinking, most popular movies fall short of *Rear Window*. This has been extensively instantiated by Noël Carroll, whose cognitive-based "question and answer" model, particularly as it pertains to suspense structures, analyses (favorably) these films' option reduction for the sake of clarity and suspense (Carroll 1996: 78–118).

According to Carroll, the power of movies to engage viewers stems from their framing of clear questions that reciprocate the expectation aroused with clear answers. Movies are pleasurable because, contrary to real-life situations, viewers get satisfactory, clear answers to all of the questions raised in the movie. Moreover, their ongoing interest is maintained by the chaining of moment-to-moment microquestions, reciprocated sooner rather than later with microanswers, along with macroquestions that are reciprocated later rather than sooner with macroanswers. In this respect, Carroll can be understood as diverging from Bordwell's suggestion that the viewers' awareness of the movie's play with their cognitive operations is what makes it pleasurable. Carroll's concern is not with whether the viewer enjoys the cognitive process, developing questions and seeking answers. His concern is rather with simplicity and clarity as the differentiating criteria between popular films-as-art and life. He goes to great lengths to show how objects in perspective-based movie images are readily identified just as we identify objects in real life, and how cinematic articulation in movies complements this simple comprehension by being mostly concerned with posing clear questions and providing clear answers through strategies of "indexing," "scaling," and "bracketing."[1] Carroll's favorable view of popular movies' reduction of vagueness and complexity to obtain clarity and simplicity is made clear in his analysis of movie suspense. Suspense, defined as uncertainty about future outcomes we care about, occurs

> when the question that arises from earlier scenes has two possible, opposed answers which have specific ratings in terms of morality and probability .... [It] results when the possible outcomes of the situation set down by the film are such that the outcome which is morally correct in terms of the values in the film is the less likely outcome (or, at least, only as likely as the evil outcome). (ibid.: 101)

The reason Carroll provides for this detected imbalance in favor of "the evil outcome" is the need to enhance the viewer's concern for the protagonist which emblematizes the preferred morality, since it arouses the viewer's concern about the uncertainty necessary for suspense.

In these respects, Carroll's model may be taken to explain the fact that most movies, particularly in suspense sequences, fall short of evoking viable optional thinking. Let me reiterate that Carroll's approach differs from Bordwell's in that it does not necessarily imply that viewers, given a question, consciously and actively turn on their implicit, ongoing, questioning process and start guessing what the answer is. As such, Carroll's position accords with my contention that optional thinking, not unlike question posing, is an ongoing, tacit, cognitive activity that needs triggering to become conscious. I would add that it also easily lends itself to manipulation when there is a heightened need for closure. Carroll's characterization of popular movies' question-and-answer model, particularly as it pertains to his analysis of suspense, seems to support the "viewer's heightened need for closure" thesis over the "hypothesizing viewer" thesis. The pleasure derived by viewers from movies has, regrettably, little to do with Bordwell's presumed guessing or hypothesizing activities in between questions and answers. Nevertheless, the simple clarity of answers or resolutions in movies does not gratify viewers on its own (Carroll), but in addition to its relief of the often distressing play of suspense and relief brought about by the "arousal boost" engendered by a heightened need for closure, and the "arousal jag" expected upon gratifying resolution.

This offers a less favorable view of movies than the one espoused by Carroll. I think that Carroll's conception of clarity and simplicity, upon which he bases his positive view of the reductive properties of movies, rests upon certain conflations and a reductive consideration of movies' cognitive affects. When these are taken into account, Carroll's esteem for these movies loses its grounding, and the conclusion can be made that narrative movies need not be reductive in order to be pleasurable, popular, or clear.

Hence, while clarity opposes vagueness and simplicity complexity, Carroll seems often to inadvertently conflate clarity with simplicity and vagueness with complexity. This seems to be the case in his suggestion that images are simply understood and therefore easy to clarify, or that suspense is more effective and clear when simplified to binary optional trajectories. While identifying objects in images may be "easier" and certainly more universal than their initial textual identification, it does not follow that within each written language, once mastered, words are not as readily and easily comprehended (the same goes for numbers). In fact, once written language is mastered, it can be more precise and clear than simple yet often vague images (that is why images are often accompanied by captions and dialogue so as to anchor their meaning). Beyond this conflation of simplicity with clarity, Carroll's reductive view of narrative suspense, whereby suspense is most effective when it outlines two strict and exclusive binary options, rests upon a conflation of vagueness with complexity and is clearly untenable. While movies do work hard to narrow the viewers' suspenseful uncertainty to two apparently binary options, this is not what their plots imply. For example, action movies focused on a fight for survival between a protagonist and an antagonist imply at least four options: either the protagonist or the antagonist lives or dies, or both live or die. Likewise, most romantic comedies include at least one of the lovers' ex-boyfriends or -girlfriends. This may result in at least four options: Either the lovers stay together or they separate, whereupon if they separate both can stay alone or one may return to his/her ex (but it can turn out that the one returning to her/his ex still keeps the new lover in a well agreed-upon arrangement, etc.). In fact, while Carroll is correct in stating that concern for a threatened protagonist enhances suspense, this does not necessarily imply binary options. It rather entails elevating the viewer's concern for the endangered protagonist along with the concomitant reduction of the antagonist to the sole function of a threat to the well-being of the protagonist. Thus, as extensively discussed in the previous section, while, in principle, movies entail several options, most popular movies ease the viewer's suspense-aroused desire for the reduction of options by repressing the inevitable, implied options embedded in every narrative.[2]

Contrary to Carroll's view, intense suspense does not depend upon the options being binary. In *Rear Window* for example, albeit faintly elaborated yet clearly detected by Bordwell, the viewer considers at least two binary-structured options as well as their causal interrelation: Will Jeff prove Thorwald killed his own wife?; Will Jeff and his girlfriend Lisa remain together?; Will Lisa lend her support to Jeff, thereby bringing them closer together and closer to proving that Thorwald killed his wife? Also, the concern for the well-being of the protagonist (and the attendant morality) do not impede the consideration of more complex portrayals of the antagonist or other characters as Carroll suggests. *Rear Window*'s suspenseful uncertainties are suspenseful only if the viewer cares about both Lisa and Jeff, despite the fact that they are often at odds and mutually threaten their well-being (e.g., their constant and often intense bickering). This rather common, popular movie complication evidences that intense suspense and gratifying closures do not depend upon the binary structure of suspense, nor that heightened concern for the protagonist impedes the consideration (under suspense) of other characters, including antagonists. What Carroll describes is less what movies do in their plot construction (though many have poor plots) and more what such movies gear their viewers to "desire." As already argued, suspense heightens the viewers' need (desire) for closure so as to relieve distressing uncertainty. However, in movie suspense the attainment of closure is delayed and determined by the movie rather than the viewer. Therefore, given their heightened need for closure, viewers tend to narrow the attribution of potential meanings for oncoming events, objects, or characters to their valence for the advancement or retardation of closure. Whenever movies allow for the binary reduction of the developing plot, or more so, when this is encouraged, movies enable the reduction of optional thinking. This is not for the sake of clarity as Carroll suggests, for complex suspense structures can be as clear (up to a point) and as suspenseful as exclusive binary options. *Rear Window* does not offer a simple plot structure and yet it is a suspenseful and very clear movie.

This view of necessary and favored reductionism is also embraced by Tan. Differing from Carroll, however, who relates this to viewers getting full and simple answers to questions as opposed to their real-life situations, Tan, well aware of the reductive cognitive affects engendered by these "emotional machines," suggests that these films are also cognitively challenging because they offer "a well timed sequence of challenges that the viewer is just barely capable of meeting" and therefore engender in viewers "the satisfaction of cognitive curiosity …[;] the sense of competence" (1996: 93). However, Tan's formulaic description of the "miracle precision" of the balanced tradeoff that popular movies engender in viewers of emotion and cognition, is not only untenable but ends up heralding the closed mindedness and optional-thinking deficiency encouraged by most movies. As Tan points out elsewhere in his book: "more cognitive effort, more satisfaction upon resolution." But "mental effort" is by definition a relative phenomenon, different in different people or for the same person at different times. Given this, it seems that Tan does not consider the consequences of his perception of the reductionism characterizing popular movies. In fact, if we take "mental effort" to be a relative phenomenon, when it is applied to movies' reductionism, it actually implies that viewers who enjoy these movies because they "can barely meet" their cognitive challenge have poor cognitive faculties. I also suspect that this approach assumes that any cognitive activity requires effort to begin with, but this is surely not the case as evidenced when our attention seems to spontaneously wander[3] (just think of the effort and training required by some oriental philosophies in order to get people to *not* think).

While cognitive-psychological approaches offer, in my view, the best available explanation and description of what most popular narrative films are all about, their almost unchecked enthusiasm for these films blocks their serious consideration of the films' powerful encouragement of closed mindedness and optional-thinking deficiency, along with the exploration of how such films, whose popularity and pleasures they so vividly hail, might encourage optional thinking without foregoing the cognitive and emotional pleasures that make them so popular. In other words, cognitive-psychological studies of film, in their accurate understanding of how these films are enjoyable, end up needlessly supporting the closed mindedness encouraged by these films as a necessary and laudable part and parcel of their pleasures.

Closed mindedness, while easy to engender through such films, is not a necessary condition of movies. In what follows I will consider in depth how some popular narrative films encourage optional thinking and open mindedness without foregoing the narrative strategies that make movies so popular.

4.2. Optional Thinking in Movies

The *sine qua non* components that account for the popularity of movies are: a challenging of the viewers' cognitive faculties in a manner that satisfyingly lets them construct a coherent story that leads to closure out of the movies' audiovisual flow; the attendant arousal, regulation, and control of a heightened need for closure, mostly through suspense-cum-surprise strategies; the evoking of empathy toward characters based upon encouraging viewers to take the characters' perspectives; and a proactive and retroactive interplay between cataphora and anaphora that imparts a sense of coherence and internal logic to the developing plot.

While these components are usually manipulated in most movies in a way that discourages optional thinking (see chapter 2), I argue that this must not necessarily be the case. It seems that lauding most such films despite their reductive approach implies a misguided and widespread conception that thinking, particularly optional thinking, is an unpleasant effort for viewers. While construing viable options within a narrative demands effort on the part of filmmakers, given the need to clearly articulate options, coordinate various points of view, maintain coherence across the narrative, and lead to closure, it is not the case that viewers cannot cognitively and emotionally enjoy following more than one option and comparing it to other options.

As already mentioned, we are optional thinkers and narrative movies are inherently optional given their loose, probabilistic causality. This suggests that narrative films, because of their depiction of apparent or feasible life situations and audiovisual flow, can offer a powerful locus for the pleasurable arousal of viable optional thinking. Hence, through audiovisually flowing narratives, films may articulate optional yet comprehensible narrative trajectories or points of view by the arrangement of these into loosely causal, audiovisually dynamic structures with a beginning, middle, and end, figuring originating events, human decisions, their complications, and their consequences. These films may lead viewers to construct, entertain, compare, and assess different points of view or optional narrative trajectories out of the films' audiovisual flow, without foregoing the components that make movies popular. In what follows I will argue this in respect of the various components that turn films into popular movies and will instantiate the argument through an analysis of some popular films and movie strategies that encourage optional thinking.

4.2.1. Optionality in Audiovisual Flow

I agree with Carroll's contention that much of the "power of movies" resides in their audiovisual clarity. That is, popular movies deploy their audiovisual framing, composition, and editing in a manner that guides the viewer's attention toward what is important in order to follow a given scene, particularly in terms of plot comprehension. However, contrary to Carroll's implication, audiovisual clarity does not necessarily mean that images have to be simple or carry a single, univocal meaning.[4] Audiovisual configuration can be clear yet complex. This complexity may result either from the editing context within which a given shot appears or from the audiovisual complexity of the shot itself. Consider for the sake of argument Kuleshov's "experiment" or "effect" whereby the close up of a person's vague expression shifts its signification retroactively depending on whether the consequent shot shows a close up of a bowl of soup ("he is hungry"), a dead child ("he is grieving"), or a seductive woman ("he is sexually aroused"). In each case the signification raised is clear and univocal. While in most movies one such signification is usually retroactively and reductively imposed, this does not have to be the case and does not exclude the possibility that the two other significations be actualized and developed. Thus, the signification of the close up may be actualized through editing so that it implies the character is hungry, grieving, and sexually aroused. This becomes evident when the shots are screened in a sequence of: bowl of soup, character's close up, dead child, character's close up, seductive woman, character's close up. In this sequence the latter shot does not exchange or exclude in a flash the previous significations and the viewer clearly maintains all three options as feasible. The same applies to complexity within a shot. This can be evidenced in a 1996 untitled photograph made by Shirin Neshat, an Iranian-born United States artist, featuring a woman's face with two fingers, inscribed with Koranic tattoos, posed over her lips. While on the one hand this gesture conveys the woman's self-silencing according to the directives of the Koran, it simultaneously conveys her kissing these Koran directives. The photograph's troubling ambivalence of sensuality and sacredness encourages two optional thoughts, emanating from the same polysemous (or rather "bisemous") photograph.

Beyond the possibility of embedding optional meanings in the audiovisual flow of single shots or movie segments, such localized optionality can be made viable when developed throughout the narrative, without foregoing narrative structure that leads to a satisfying closure (or closures) and while using suspense, surprise, empathy for characters, and the coherence established by the anaphora–cataphora interplay.

4.2.2. Movies Encouraging Optional Thinking

Films encouraging optional thinking can be divided into two broad categories. One consists of films that include alternative narrative tracks, closures, and perspectives within the fictional world of the movie, while the other category subsumes some films that meaningfully recall, for some viewers, alternative narrative tracks that are external to the movie and can be constructed by these viewers as optional.

In my analysis of movies with optional narrative tracks and closures (*Sliding Doors* and *Run Lola Run*) I will show in particular that viewers can follow two or three alternate narrative trajectories leading to different closures in a manner that strongly cues optional thinking. The analysis suggests that this is achieved because viewers are given enough information to construct the alternate narrative tracks in their minds, and because these alternate tracks can be compared and assessed in a comprehensive manner due to a convergence achieved by the use of constants across tracks, and a divergence stemming from variables. The analysis of these films also shows that viewers can, if required for the overall comprehension of the movie, easily follow, compare, and assess these alternative tracks while being in suspense or when facing surprise. Actually, the added cognitive effort when in suspense enhances the enjoyment of these films while the experience of surprise triggers rather than blocks the generation of hypotheses embedded in surprising situations. This is because surprises in these movies do not force an exclusion of previously suggested alternate hypotheses as false to the fiction (as is the case in *The Sixth Sense*) but lead viewers to compare how a surprise stemming from a variable in one alternative track shifts the course of events, while maintaining, as true to the fiction, the parallel variable and its outcome in the other, alternate track. This counters a common cognitive-psychological presumption that movies must be simple and reductive of options to be comprehensible during suspense or surprise.

In an analysis of *Rashomon*, I will focus upon how overlapping character perspectives can powerfully cue optional thinking in viewers if empathy is not restricted to the leading protagonist (as is the case in most movies) but is evoked for all characters by encouraging the viewer to alternately take their respective perspectives. I will also discuss how in *Rashomon* coherence can be forged through an anaphora–cataphora interplay that does not force an anaphoric, retroactive reduction of cataphors to a univocal meaning as in most movies. In *Rashomon*, the cataphora–anaphora interplay encourages optional thinking rather than blocks it because the anaphoric, retroactive attribution of meaning to preceding cataphors does not force an exclusion of their previously suggested meanings as false or irrelevant to the fiction (as is the case in *The Sixth Sense*). It rather leads viewers to assess how its polysemy is respectively meaningful to different characters.

In an analysis of films that recall alternative, fictional, narrative tracks that are external to the movie (e.g., *Alice in Wonderland*'s recall of Lewis Carroll's *Alice's Adventures in Wonderland*), I argue that the cueing of optional thinking in these movies is more volatile due to the enhancement of extraneous factors. I then discuss under what terms they may cue optional thinking in some viewers, suggesting among other reasons that this may occur to viewers who are familiar with the referenced text and when the movie alternative stems from, and is grounded upon options embedded but not materialized in the originating version. Such works may not only encourage some viewers' optional thinking, but do so by unraveling the embedded optionality inhering in the originating fiction.

Finally, in an analysis of films that recall alternative, historical, narrative tracks (e.g., *Inglourious Basterds* recalls World War II), I will consider in particular the issue of historical truth as a possible impediment to the cueing of optional thinking. I suggest that when a movie readily conforms to a known historical trajectory it short-circuits optional thinking, whereas when it offers a counterfactual "history" it may block optional thinking for those offended by the transgression of historical facts. However, if the alternative, counterfactual history flaunts its fictional nature it may encourage powerful optional thinking in viewers, suggesting that the course of history is not predetermined and that different, alternative futures can always ensue.

4.2.2.1. Movies with Optional Narrative Tracks: *Run Lola Run* and *Sliding Doors*

Films using optional narrative tracks or "forking path narratives" (Bordwell 2002)[5] can offer consecutive or parallel well structured narrative trajectories that in their converging and diverging interrelations lead to alternative yet coherent and feasible closures. This is evidenced in the popular, suspenseful, narrative films *Run Lola Run* and *Sliding Doors*. *Run Lola Run* offers the viewer three consecutive versions of the same suspenseful and fast-tracked story, having to do with Lola's (Franka Potente) urgent need to gather DM 100,000 for her boyfriend, Manni (Moritz Bleibtreu), in twenty minutes. If she fails then Manni will most probably be killed by a crook he works for and whose money he has lost. Each version ends differently (in the first Lola alone is killed, in the second only Manni is killed, and in the third they both get away with the money). These differing closures result from the different obstacles Lola encounters, or different decisions she makes as she runs across Berlin to get to Manni on time. Likewise, in *Sliding Doors*, two parallel, intertwined versions of the life of Helen Quilley (Gwyneth Paltrow) are offered, splitting off at a point where she misses or boards the same train as James (John Hannah), a man she has just met. Throughout the film we see what would have happened in each version. When she catches the train, she and charming James get acquainted and when Helen gets home she finds her boyfriend Gerry (John Lynch) in bed with another woman, an event that eventually leads her towards a happy life with James. However, in the version where she misses the train, she also misses finding out about Gerry's infidelity and ends up living a miserable life.

Bordwell (2002) has clearly shown how the structure shared by these movies, of optional narrative tracks, allows viewers to comprehensibly follow the alternative narrative threads undertaken by the same characters and leading them into different destinies in each narrative path.[6] He calls these kinds of films "forking path" films, a phrase borrowed from Borges' story *The Garden of Forking Paths*, which is often mentioned by postmodern narrative theorists as one of their foundational stories. However, Bordwell rejects the feasibility of constructing a film based on Borges' labyrinth story that consists of "an infinite series of times, a growing, dizzying web of divergent, convergent, and parallel times ... that approach one another, fork, are snipped off" (ibid.: 88). His argument is that while a story such as this might be imagined, it cannot be made into a film a viewer can follow and comprehend and that consequently, "in fiction, alternative futures seem pretty limited affairs" (ibid.: 89).[7] Attendant to this requirement to restrict options in favour of comprehensibility, Bordwell further points out that in movies with optional narrative tracks,

> narrative patterning obligingly highlights a single crucial incident and traces out its inevitable implications. Instead of each moment being equally pregnant with numerous futures, one becomes far more consequential than the others, and those consequences will follow strictly from it. Such linearity helps make these plots intelligible, yielding two or three stories that illustrate, literally, alternative but integral courses of events. (ibid.: 92)

Hence, rather than the unfeasible narrative possibility of shifting among narrative threads at any point or many different points, a project bound to lead to gaming distraction or cognitive confusion, these films offer transitions between narrative tracks at narrative junctures that are highlighted as crucial, such as the train's sliding doors in *Sliding Doors* or the two tragic closures in *Run Lola Run*.

Bordwell also analyses how, for the sake of viewer interest and comprehensibility, the different narrative tracks in these films are interrelated through various cohering strategies, such as the play of constancy and variation upon the same temporal and spatial trajectories, the recurrence of some actions, and the use of the same characters in the alternative versions, allowing the viewer to construe meaningful interrelations between the different threads, including attention to overarching thematic or formal concerns. Indeed, *Run Lola Run* repeats in succession three different options within the same basic story, keeping the characters, most locales, and events the same, as well as the overall narrative evolution, whereas *Sliding Doors* runs two such options in parallel.[8]

Bordwell detects further strategies used by these films to forge in viewers a notion of a coherent, temporal, dramatic succession of events that leads to closure, a notion that may be easily lost in films that shift between alternative or optional narrative tracks that lead to different outcomes. In particular he finds in these films the inclusion within each narrative track of a shared crucial juncture that sets time constraints, as in *Run Lola Run*, where the three narrative versions start with the same phone call by Lola's boyfriend Manni, in which he sets the suspenseful twenty-minute time frame for her to save him. This repeated temporal constraint not only frames a suspense trajectory but also imparts a notion of dramatic succession in between the different narrative threads, despite their separate and consecutively evolving time frame. Another related strategy, involving what I have termed the anaphora–cataphora interplay, is used in *Sliding Doors* when toward the end, the film flashes back and reenacts a choice event that happened before Helen missed the train. In this reenacted choice event, we are reminded that in her initial encounter with James, he picked up an earring that she had dropped. Initially, Helen refused to recognize his behavior as flirting, whereas this time around she accepts it. This makes her missing of the train irrelevant. Thus, as Bordwell puts it, the movie "lets its epilogue fold back on its prologue" (2002: 101). This strategy anaphorically recouches an inadvertent encounter, turning this encounter in retrospect into a cataphora. This strategy not only imparts a sense of dramatic succession in between the parallel optional narrative tracks but also suggests a preference for the happy rather than the sad ending by "short circuiting" intermediary narrative developments. Bordwell suggests that this return, happening toward the end of the movie, caters to the viewers' psychological "*recency* effect" (ibid.: 100) predisposition that imparts salience to the most recent impression, retrospectively framing previous threads according to it and highlighting the final, happy movie closure. Moreover, since this return anaphorically recalls a scene from the film's beginning, it reconnects to the viewer's psychological predisposition of primacy that imparts salience to the first impressions. Thus, the strategy of returning to and actualizing an event from early in the movie interconnects the "primacy effect" in viewers with the "recency effect," thus forging the psychological sense of overall coherence expected from narratives. As Bordwell puts it:

> A narrative, in Meir Sternberg's formulation, involves telling in time, and as a time-bound process, it calls upon a range of human psychological propensities. What comes earlier shapes our expectations about what follows. What comes later modifies our understanding of what went before; retrospection is often as important as prospection. (ibid.: 97–98)

Bordwell's overall accurate detection and analysis of the narrative strategies used by these movies to allow viewer comprehension underestimates their evocation of viable optional thinking. Being more concerned with how these movies present a mere variation upon regular movies, Bordwell implies that they eliminate or end up blocking the potential for optional thinking, and that there is nothing qualitatively different in them. This view is evident in his use of terms such as "inevitable outcomes" and "strict" consequences when describing these movies' causality in the narrative trajectories outlined between transitional junctures; in his apparent downgrading of the films' philosophical consistency in that from this point of view, the highlighting of one event over others as being "pregnant with numerous futures" is arbitrary; and particularly in his implication that constants between narrative tracks, shared suspenseful time constraints, and the exploitation of primacy and recency effects on viewers gear viewers toward the "short-circuiting" and psychological obliteration of all options but the salient last option and closure, which he claims becomes the most "plausible" option.

However, Bordwell's implication is unwarranted and overlooks the inherent evocation of optional thinking in viewers by these movies. As has already been discussed, narrative causality is always probable rather than "inevitable" or "strict." While regular movies work hard to forge an apparent sense of inevitability, this must surely fail in films with different linear tracks that recount the same story in different versions. Such films, in their overlay of options, bring forth to the viewers' attention the inherent probabilistic and optional nature of narrative causality within and across the alternative narrative tracks. This is due to the fact that the viewer is compelled to compare these different tracks in order to comprehend them, a comparison that necessarily entails awareness of optional and probabilistic narrative causality. This is recurrently emphasized in such films. In *Run Lola Run*, for example, each version of the story is shorter than the last, compelling the viewer to memorize the preceding version in order to understand what is going on. Likewise, probabilistic causality and optionality are recurrently emphasized in the presentation of identical events that engender different outcomes in different versions, compelling the viewer to compare and evaluate them (e.g., when Lola in all three versions brushes the same passerby as she runs, each such encounter generates a brief sequence of rushing stills portraying a different potential life trajectory for the passerby). What is important in the probabilistic causality characterizing each narrative trajectory in between transitional junctures is not its apparently inevitable failure, but its turning each optional narrative track into a viable option for viewers to consider.

Moreover, the overall variation upon constants (characters, locale, events, etc.) is not only for the sake of comprehensibility as Bordwell maintains, but primarily aimed at focusing the viewer upon the optionality of these films. Thus, while in regular movies optionality may be presumed in the replication or variation of options through different characters (e.g., in many romantic comedies or dramas the main couple's relationship trajectory is often countered or replicated in a minor trajectory figuring a different couple), viewers do not necessarily comprehend these other characters as variations on or alternatives to the leading protagonists because the presumed alternative is carried out by different and usually minor characters, within different situations and locales. Thus, such presumed variations in most movies are inherently considered as unique[9] rather than viably optional. Conversely, in optional movies the variation of constants compels viewers to consider and compare the different trajectories as optional.

Also, while the highlighting of certain events over others as transitional junctures is perhaps philosophically unwarranted as Bordwell suggests, such highlighting is not unwarranted at all in terms of the viewers' narrative-construction process, as it enhances the viewer's viable optional thinking. This is because the narrative junctures that transition the plot from one trajectory to a parallel, alternate trajectory encourage the notion of happenstance or choice in life without foregoing the viewer's process of knowledge construction. Moreover, such transitions, because of their own and the movie's overall invocation of probabilistic causality, meaningfully suggest the idea that any other point in the movie may be also fraught with possible futures. Furthermore, in these movies, crucial transitional junctures are usually placed at dramatic crossroads construed in such a manner that they guide the viewer to expect and accept the "what if?" optionality suggested in the transitional juncture. A meaningful "what if?" process is encouraged because these films offer a coherent, suspenseful, dramatic build up toward these narrative-track transition junctures, and a coherent and suspenseful follow up to them in the alternate option. In *Run Lola Run* the viewer wishes for a different closure in the first two versions upon learning that Lola and Manni respectively have been killed. Such closures enhance the viewer's willingness to entertain as feasible the "what if?" optional conjectures offered in the succeeding versions, each reframing in an alternate narrative track a coherent and suspenseful follow up to this juncture. Likewise, in *Sliding Doors* it is the suspenseful *return* to a crucial transitional juncture in the movie's diegetic past that predisposes the viewer to expect and accept the retrospective suggestion that things could have turned out differently. This enhances the viewer's "what if?" thoughts of the type "if only that had not happened!" or "if only the character had decided to take a different course of action!" When Helen misses the train and consequently fails to discover that her boyfriend, Gerry, is cheating on her, the viewer, who knows what Helen does not, expects and wishes for her to embrace the flirtation of James, who runs into her by chance (an event that prefigures the interlacing of both versions, an interlacing that in itself compels optional thinking). This expectation, thwarted in what follows, predisposes the viewer to accept the film's potential fulfillment of this wish when returning to the juncture of the train's sliding doors, and to expect in suspense the resolutions to the parallel "what if?" options ensuing from this bifurcation. This expectation is then gratifyingly reciprocated by the splitting of the movie into two viable, optional developments and two viable closures.

These suspenseful films also subvert the widespread assumption that the viewer will feel uncomfortable or will find it hard to follow experiencing more than one option when in suspense. This idea presumes that the viewer has a one-track mind rather than realizing that it is the movie that encourages this kind of restricted thinking.[10] In other words, suspense constructs need not be geared toward a tight, linear, and single closure to be pleasurable. While audiovisual flow and suspense heighten the viewers' need for closure and thereby gear them toward cognitive reductionism, the attendant arousal of their fear of invalid comprehension may gear them toward enhanced attention to incoming information. If this enhanced attention compels viewers to entertain more than one option and if these options are viably developed and interrelated so that coherence and closure are established within and across options, viewers will attentively follow and entertain these optional narrative developments.

There is no ground for accepting Bordwell's suggestion that these movies exploit the viewers' psychological predisposition for primacy-recency, which cancels out optionality. While primacy and recency predispositions may aid the notion of coherence, these only suggest, in optional movies, that the last optional closure is the one preferred by the movie (or the viewers, as in the happy ending of both *Run Lola Run* and *Sliding Doors*). Bordwell's position seems to stem from the usual manipulation of the cataphora–anaphora interplay in nonoptional movies to forge an apparent sense of strict and inevitable narrative causality. But in the optional movies discussed, the sense of coherence imparted through their anaphora–cataphora interplay reinforces rather than diminishes optionality. While Bordwell takes this recouching to imply the "short-circuiting" of the sad option, he overlooks the fact that the anaphoric recouching of this event *shifts* its original cataphoric meaning, thus turning this first encounter into a crucial choice and decision point by the overlay in the viewer's memory of both the first and second presentations of this first encounter. Thus, rather than "short-circuiting" the parallel, sad trajectory, it is only because it is as plausible and viable as the other, happy one that viewers, after assessing both options, prefer the happy ending.

There is no good cause to accept Bordwell's attempt to force these movies into being a mere variation of regular, nonoptional movies. As my analysis shows, *Run Lola Run* and *Sliding Doors* are exemplary popular films that encourage optional thinking in viewers.

4.2.2.2. Overlapping Perspectives: *Rashomon*

Another major narrative strategy evoking viable optional thinking concerns encouraging viewers to take different character perspectives and coordinate them. This may occur if the empathy of the viewer is not constrained to a single protagonist and his/her outlook, and if this overlay of outlooks compels the viewer to interlace, assess, and compare them for narrative comprehension.

An exemplary case evidencing this strategy is Akira Kurosawa's masterpiece *Rashomon*. Set in eleventh-century Japan, the movie shows the contradictory versions of an event through flashbacks that are narrated by unreliable witnesses, whereby a notorious outlaw named Tajōmaru (Toshirō Mifune) has apparently raped a samurai's wife (Machiko Kyō) and consequently killed the samurai (Masayuki Mori). The first three contradicting versions, offered consequently by Tajōmaru, the woman, and the dead samurai— "transmitted" through a clairvoyant medium (Fumiko Honma)—

are given before an unseen judge, whose point of view corresponds to that of the viewer. Each version includes a flashback to the event, presented from the perspective of the teller.

First, Tajōmaru admits to killing the samurai and to raping the woman but claims that the woman began to desire him and then begged him to kill her husband to avoid shame. He then released the samurai and killed him in a fair and honorable sword duel. When he turned around the woman was gone and he stupidly forgot to take with him the woman's valuable dagger.

The woman then tells her story: she was raped by Tajōmaru who then fled the scene. Distressed, she ran toward her husband, who was tied up and gave her a cold and disgusted look. Shamed, she released him and pleaded with him to kill her with her own dagger, but with an insulting and dismissing look he declined. She ran away to a river where she tried to kill herself but failed. Then she fainted. When she returned she found her husband slain by her own dagger.

In the slain Samurai's version, the woman, after succumbing to Tajōmaru, incited Tajōmaru to kill him. Upon hearing this, Tajōmaru asked the samurai whether to kill the shameless woman, an offer the samurai respected but declined. Then the woman fled the scene chased by Tajōmaru, who returned after a few hours empty handed. While releasing the samurai, Tajōmaru told him before leaving that his wife would probably tell everybody about what had transpired. In his humiliation, the samurai noticed the discarded dagger which he used to take his own life. As he lay dying, he felt someone pulling the dagger out of his body. These three versions are themselves recounted in a flashback by a woodcutter (Takashi Shimura) who found the body and reported it to the authorities, and by a priest (Minoru Chiaki) who saw the couple in the woods before the crime. Since they are both present in court, their versions seem objective. They tell the stories to a commoner (Kichijiro Ueda) who joins them under the huge and ruined Rashomon Gate where they find shelter from the incessant heavy rain. After each version has been recounted, the movie returns to the Rashomon site and the woodcutter comments that his testimony was deceitful. Following the third version the woodcutter suddenly says he actually witnessed the event but did not report it for fear of getting involved with the authorities. In his version the woman, after angrily refusing Tajōmaru's pleading that she marry him, ran in despair and released her tied-up husband so the men could decide her fate. However, when the samurai refused to fight Tajōmaru for an "unworthy woman," she rose from the ground and in uncontrolled despair started humiliating both men for fearing the fight. This and their hidden affection for the woman led both of them to hesitatingly engage each other, both being scared to death. Eventually, Tajōmaru killed the samurai and turned, exhausted, toward the woman, who escaped in horror. Then Tajōmaru slowly and regretfully retreated, holding his sword and the sword he drew out from the samurai's body.

After the woodcutter recounts his version, the commoner comments that it is as deceitful as the others because the woodcutter (whom we know has already lied once to the authorities) apparently stole the valuable dagger from the scene of the murder. In the concluding scene, the priest comments how he is depressed by the deceitful and self-interested nature of all those involved in the event. This includes for him the woodcutter who admits stealing the dagger, and the commoner who just stole a blanket and an amulet from a baby they found abandoned amidst the ruins. However, the priest regains his faith in humanity upon learning that the woodcutter intends to take the abandoned baby home with him and raise him along with his own six children.

Rashomon gradually compels us to compare the versions in order to decipher the truth from the contradictions and overlapping portions of the differing accounts. This, however, cannot result in a definite conclusion, both because all versions are told by unreliable narrators,[11] including the woodcutter's last version, and because even in a retrospective analysis the true story cannot be construed. This has led commentators on the movie (including Kurosawa) to focus upon the movie's themes of unreliability, of the impossibility to uncover the truth given human subjectivity, and of the need people have to portray themselves in a favorable way. Thus, Tajōmaru's version underlines his concern with how manly he is in respect of his conquering women and his skillful and fair swordfighting; the woman's is concerned with her chastity and loyalty; the samurai's with his honor (or what the "medium" perceives as his honor); and the woodcutter's with human fear, weakness, and the need for repentance which he projects upon all others.

Notwithstanding this theme, which has turned the movie title into a concept used in different fields to describe confounding and irresolvable accounts of an event, what concerns us here is the powerful way in which this movie encourages optional thinking in its viewers. This is initially due to the strategy of compelling viewers to interlace and compare the different versions for comprehension, through their attempt to uncover the (unreachable) truth.

However, had this been the major strategy, aim, and viewer affect of the movie, it could have encouraged a loopy type of optionality, given that the truth-search is dead ended, thereby engendering upon conclusion a sense of helpless defeat.[12] Yet, such interpretation and loopy thinking cannot be comprehensibly attributed to the movie and its overall experience. It cannot explain away, for example, the fact that the movie ends with a reaffirmation of human conscientiousness and a belief in simple honesty. This viably transpires through the woodcutter's apparent realization that his past deeds (theft, and perhaps murder) and his consequent lies need not determine, and may even encourage, another viable trajectory for him based on compassion and honesty. This is evidenced in the woodcutter's admission of his theft to the priest and his consequent passionate deed toward the abandoned baby.

This interlacing, while propelled by the viewer's search for truth, is more important for our concern in that it directs the viewer toward taking a comparative approach to the different perspectives of the characters in terms of their respective viable, subjective concerns within the shared event. This major viewer concern is achieved through evoking the viewers' empathy toward each character within his/her own narrated version and by framing each version from the perspective of the narrator.

Hence, the flashbacks begin with the one giving testimony seated in the foreground and facing an unseen and unheard judge, whose point of view corresponds to that of the viewer.[13] This semidirect address calls upon the viewers to judge the characters, while also engendering gradual empathy for them. This empathy is enhanced when, throughout the flashback, the viewer is occasionally returned visually to this setting, or aurally, through the overlay of the narrating character's voice over the flashback shots. In these returns the character tells of his/her inner thoughts at certain moments shown in the flashback, thus further deepening our understanding of the character and consequently enhancing our empathy for him/her. Also, different events within the flashback are mostly shown from the character's point of view. Thus, as the flashback progresses, the viewers' perception of the events from the perspective of the narrating character encourages the viewer to feel empathy toward that character.[14]

The structuring of each flashback as a suspenseful story heightens the viewers' need for closure, predisposing them to expect and accept the flashback's resolution along with the outlook of the character propelling it. Thus, upon comparing the different versions and the gradual realization that none is true, the viewer is left with the comparative assessment of the differing yet viable outlooks of the characters s/he empathizes with. While being concerned with whether and how Tajōmaru lies, the viewer gradually takes a liking even toward this rapist and killer, by coming to understand what motivates him (to conquer women but also to gain their respect, and to be a skillful, honorable warrior). Furthermore, as the movie progresses from flashback to flashback, the viewer compiles optional portrayals of the characters. Hence, while the woodcutter's flashback is oriented by his need to project upon others his own fear, weakness, and need for repentance, it also imparts another feasible option for comprehending Tajōmaru, because in this version, repentant Tajōmaru is seen begging the woman he now loves to marry him, promising her to amend his ways and even get a decent job.

The consecutive overlapping perspectives are held by an anaphora–cataphora interplay that lends coherence to the story, but this coherence is not based upon an apparent sense of strict narrative, but rather a flaunted probabilistic causality. This is because all versions are tentative and probabilistic, thereby lending each cataphora a revised anaphoric meaning that does not cancel out its previous optional meanings. Thus, in Tajōmaru's version the woman's dagger symbolizes her submission, for after waving it to resist the rape, when taken by Tajōmaru she lets it fall to the ground as her passion for him grows. Within this version, the dagger's symbolization is later anaphorically couched as cataphora for Tajōmaru's disrespect for the woman, for when asked in court what happened to the dagger he says he forgot all about it, just as he has previously said he forgot the woman once he had raped her. However, in the woman's version the dagger is anaphorically recouched as something that she wants to be used to affirm her loyalty to her husband, which is implied in her asking him to kill her with it when he mocks her chastity. While these symbols of the dagger contradict each other, they are not mutually exclusive for the viewers for they maintain throughout the rest of the movie these three options (and others) as viable (e.g., submission, neglect, loyalty).

Finally, *Rashomon*, despite using toward the end the strategy of surprise within a suspense structure, does not exclude all previous options as false. Differing from most movies using this strategy to block optional thinking (see the analysis above of *The Sixth Sense* and *The Ghost Writer*), the woodcutter's sudden and surprising revelation that he actually witnessed the whole event, a surprising disclosure enhanced by the expectation for the "true" version concerning the event, does not exclude our assessment of previous versions as viable. This is because right before his second version (the first being that he found the body) the commoner immediately says to him "so, your evidence at court was a lie." Moreover, after the woodcutter's new version is over, the commoner comments that it is as unreliable as all others, for he probably stole the missing dagger from the scene. Finally, the woodcutter admits to the priest that he stole the dagger, leading the viewer to reassess the woodcutter's perspective upon events alongside all previous perspectives rather than as the privileged or even "true" version.

Through such popular movie strategies, *Rashomon* encourages optional thinking in its viewers. It does this by gearing them toward comparing the viable optional outlooks of different characters on a shared event, as well as by comparing the optional outlooks on each character, as provided by how this character is viably seen from the point of view of other characters.

I would like to return in conclusion to the claim implied in the writings of some commentators on the movie, whereby this latter strategy is achieved in *Rashomon* by framing consecutive, shifting perspectives on a character within the relativity of subjectivity, thus implying that all perspectives might be wrong in relation to the always evasive truth about past events. However, as discussed above, *Rashomon* evades the loopy thinking that such subjective relativity might engender in some viewers, by shifting the woodcutter's perspective toward the end and having him perform a deed that is true within the fiction. This undisputed true and compassionate deed (his adopting the abandoned baby) further lends retroactive viability to the previous perspectives of all characters. Given this undisputed truth, it comes back to mind, as was the case throughout the movie, that while some may have totally or partly lied, others may have not. It is not the case that if you have different, contradictory versions they are thereby all false, or that the truth may never be revealed or approximated in cases where versions are conflicting. Therefore, despite the fact that in *Rashomon* we cannot find out what exactly transpired, we can assume that beyond the fact that all versions are feasible and account for the known facts, all are partially true (at least where they coincide) and some *may* be fully true or false.

Moreover, and more important for our concern with viable optional thinking, given the woodcutter's change of heart, we are driven to entertain the option that all other characters could have changed their perspective upon things and changed the course they have taken in their life toward alternative futures. Such options reverberate throughout the movie. Thus, the woodcutter's description of Tajōmaru as repenting his way of life may have been the result of the woodcutter's imaginary projection, but it may also be a feasible course for Tajōmaru to take in possible alternate futures. He can also be considered not responsible for the killing despite his bragging admittance to it, given the testimony offered by the samurai through the "medium," and given that the woman testified it was her dagger rather than Tajōmaru's sword that killed him. Likewise, if there is an afterlife, as is suggested by the movie, the samurai might rest in peace upon realizing through his wife's testimony that she was violated against her will and still loves him, whereas she may have indeed run away with Tajōmaru as suggested by the samurai's "medium," as it is highly unlikely that Tajōmaru, being so close to her, could not catch her, contrary to what he told the samurai when releasing him.

Contrary to attempts at comprehending *Rashomon* as a "loopy thinking" type of movie and the attendant loss of confidence in reaching the truth or in the viability of changing one's life, *Rashomon*, in placing the overlapping perspectives within the framework of a renewed confidence in humans that is true to the fiction, encourages again the commendable values of searching for the truth and of the feasibility of choice and change in one's life.

In what follows I will briefly consider other types of movies that may encourage optional thinking in their narrative structure without recourse to the overlay of optional narrative tracks, perspectives, or closures within the movie.

4.2.2.3. Movies with Narrative Alternatives to Previous Works of Fiction: *Belle de Jour* and *Alice in Wonderland*

One major evocation of viable optional thinking in movies requires that alternative options carry enough information to be construed by viewers into viable alternative narratives in a manner that gears them toward comparing and assessing the alternatives. I further suggest here that such gearing in movies can be attained if viewers are compelled to consciously assess probable alternatives that are internal to the fiction in order to comprehend it. In other words, given the structure and psychological affects that make movies popular, particularly the heightened need for closure encouraged by suspense, the predominance of attention to the fictional illusion (Gombrich 1969), the expectation for uniqueness (Gerrig 1993), and the need to avoid split attention and distraction (Chandler and Sweller 1991), if viewers are not compelled to assess probable alternatives within the fictional world they will focus their attention upon the most probable and viable fictional option at hand, ignoring any others, as this option is the one promoted within the fiction. This is why, while in principle every popular narrative trajectory is optional and is comprehended based upon previous knowledge that is external to the fiction at hand, viewers, when experiencing the fiction, usually bracket off such previous knowledge or transmute it into the fiction at hand, focusing moment-by-moment upon the fictional "internal probabilities" (N. Carroll 1996b: 81). These propositions usually have more valence within the fiction than external knowledge we might have.[15] As Carroll puts it, "This notion of internal probability is crucial to specifying the content of what the audience is to imagine in the course of consuming a suspense fiction ... [:] we know that *In the Dessert* is by Karl May, but we do not imagine that as part of what is to follow the story. It is not part of the story, nor should it be part of our imaginative response to the story" (ibid.).[16] This is one major reason why intertextual decoding based upon an open intertextuality does not usually entail optional thinking by viewers.

Nevertheless, when a movie offers a specific narrative option to an "originating" (Ben-Porath 1993) yet external narrative work of fiction, in a manner that the movie alternative stems from and is grounded upon options embedded but not materialized in the originating version, optional thinking may ensue for those familiar with the referenced text. Such works not only encourage optional thinking in some viewers but do so by unraveling the embedded optionality inhering in the originating fiction.

Among movies that encourage optional thinking in this manner there are parodies where we are compelled to draw upon the originating text for comprehension, evaluating the parody in respect of the alternative it provides to the originating text. These works, however, are usually perceived as a reductive caricature of one single streak within the originating text. *Austin Powers: The Spy Who Shagged Me*, for example, cannot be fully comprehended without recourse to the James Bond movies it stems from. Its (self-effacing) critique of the Manichean world of the parodied films cannot be understood by solely focusing on the nostalgic 1960s, hippie-styled, ugly agent. This parody ultimately fails to suggest a comprehensive viable alternative to the Bond series because of its inconsistent alteration of the image of the secret agent. Austin Powers (Mike Myers), beyond being ugly and styled as a hippie, is competent and triumphant over (Dr) evil, as Bond is over the original yet similarly comic evil characters of *Dr. No* (Terence Young 1962) or *Goldfinger* (Guy Hamilton 1964).

A more viable alternative can be found in what Ziva Ben-Porath (1993) terms "pseudo-metonymical allusions"; that is, texts that while seemingly identical to their originating text critically revise the latter. Such texts both compel viewers to compare the new work in respect of the original it subverts, while also realizing the viable alternative offered.[17]

A good example of this strategy is Luis Buñuel's *Belle de Jour* (1967). The film is an adaptation of Joseph Kessel's book written in 1928 and carrying the same title. Buñuel, however, in the adaptation process, critiques the book by changing the code determining the combination of materials. The film, like the book, tells the story of Severine (Catherine Deneuve), a bourgeois woman who loves her husband (Jean Sorel) but is sexually unsatisfied. Following a hint given her by one of their friends (Michel Piccoli) she arrives at a brothel and starts working there during the daytime hours when her husband is busy at work, finding sexual satisfaction in a series of weird sexual encounters with different clients. However, her guilty feelings toward her betrayed yet beloved husband, along with the chance encounter she has in the brothel with the friend who told her about the place and is surprised to see her there, lead to her having delusions where she is punished for her "sins." Things are further complicated when a young and handsome delinquent (Pierre Clémenti) pays a visit to the brothel and falls in love with her. He starts demanding that they meet outside the brothel and when she refuses he arrives at her house. When asked to leave he decides to await the return of her husband and shoots him, leaving the husband mute and paralysed. Escaping, the delinquent crashes into a car, gets into a shootout with a police officer and is shot dead. Sometime later, the friend (Michel Piccoli) pays a visit to the paralysed husband and tells him about his wife's conduct. Following this, the woman loses touch with reality. In the film's final scene the husband rises from his wheelchair and joins his wife for a drink on the terrace from which they see a horse-drawn carriage that figured in the woman's early delusions.

The book's code is based on a clear distinction between reality and delusion, which supports its distinction between virtuous marital love and immoral sexual desire. Buñuel, however, dismantled the distinction between reality and delusion, thereby collapsing the moral distinction. He did this by shifting almost unnoticeably between reality and delusion. Hence, besides delusions clearly marked as such through disjointed editing and symbolism, which occur in a space different from the Parisian milieu of the "reality" portions of the film (e.g., a disjointedly edited scene where a horse-drawn carriage drives Severine into the woods, she is tied, half-naked, to a tree, mud is thrown over her white dress, and slurs are shouted at her), there are also delusions that occur in her regular "reality," her Parisian milieu, edited in continuity (e.g., a scene where the woman sits with her husband and their friend in an outdoor café when all of a sudden the friend breaks a wine bottle and crouches with the woman underneath the table. The husband, who remains seated by the table, says he does not understand their murmurings). Likewise, there are delusions that occur in the "delusional" space but are built like another continuous reality scene, where the woman meets a new weird client (e.g., a "realistic"-looking and continuously edited scene where she meets a client in a café who asks her to play his dead wife but then calls for the horse-drawn carriage that figured in her delusions, causing doubt as to the nature of the carriage: whether it's "real" or another "delusion"). A similar confounding of reality and delusion occurs in other registers, such as when characters say things like, "the sun is black today," or when at one point, without apparent narrative reasoning, a shot of the woman's Parisian apartment building is superimposed upon a shot of the woods from her delusions. The final confusion occurs in the last scene where, as noted above, her suddenly rehabilitated husband joins her in their Parisian apartment's terrace, but what they see below is the horse-drawn carriage passing through the woods from her delusions.

Buñuel's change of the book's code collapses the book's moral and objective distinction between virtuous, asexual, marital love and punishable, debased, sexual desire, offering instead the option whereby such a dichotomy engenders maddening consequences that result in the commingling of reality and delusion. While Buñuel's movie maintains the book's suspense structure in that we are concerned with how Severine will surmount the complication arising from the collision between her secret and overt lives, the overlay of this suspense structure in the book and the film (for those familiar with the book) compels a comparative assessment of the book's morality with Buñuel's subversion of this morality in suggesting it leads toward insanity.

A similar strategy can be found in Tim Burton's three-dimensional movie *Alice in Wonderland* (2010), a version of Lewis Carroll's book *Alice's Adventures in Wonderland* (1865). In this movie, Linda Woolverton's script forges a Disney-style linear and causally logical story out of Carroll's nonsense-logic-based book. On the one hand, the movie offers a loyal and visually powerful three-dimensional rendition of the original fantasy in terms of the characters, the settings, the abundance of logical puns, and most of the events and their order of appearance. On the other hand, the movie forges out of these elements a suspenseful trajectory that culminates in a final battle between the good and the bad queens, whereupon Alice (Maya Wasikowska) and the Mad Hatter (Johnny Depp) help kill the evil Red Queen (Helena Bonham Carter). This narrative compels the viewer to compare its linear, suspenseful trajectory with the book's scrambled temporality. Furthermore, in the movie, presented as a sequel to the book, Alice, now a young woman about to enter into an arranged marriage to someone she dislikes, reenters her seven-year-old fantasy world to reemerge as a triumphant and independent woman who refuses the marriage arrangement. Thus, Carroll's childlike, scrambled fantasy, that offers and remains to the end an alternative to commonsense, adult, orderly logic, shifts its meaning through its suspenseful narrative trajectory and turns into a *Bildungsroman* based on the overcoming of obstacles that lead to grownup independence. This fundamental shift, however, does not substitute the original perception of the fantasy but rather offers it an optional explanation that compels the viewers who know the book to compare and assess both options. This is not only because of the shared elements between both texts, but mostly because Burton's option is suggested, yet not materialized within Carroll's book, which ultimately maintains the fantasy as a childhood option that does not function as a mechanism for growing up. Thus, for example, the book concludes with Alice's sister's thoughts after having heard Alice's fantasy dream:

> Lastly, she pictured to herself how this same little sister of hers would, in the after-time, be herself a grown woman; and how she would keep, through all her riper years, the simple and loving heart of her childhood: and how she would gather about her other little children, and make THEIR eyes bright and eager with many a strange tale, perhaps even with the dream of Wonderland of long ago: and how she would feel with all their simple sorrows, and find a pleasure in all their simple joys, remembering her own child-life, and the happy summer days. (Carroll 2009: 101)

Interestingly, many viewers acquainted with the book judged the optional version of the movie to be a forgery, a poor and unacceptable rendition of the original.[18] I would like to suggest that such reaction to the movie, while stemming from an assessment of its optional nature, does not encourage optional thinking in these viewers because they perceive it as violating an important belief of theirs concerning the need to protect the original version. For these viewers, the book as "external" and sacred information manages to delegitimate the fictional probabilities internal to the movie fiction (e.g., will Alice manage or fail to defeat the Red Queen?) as a viable alternative to the original. I suggest that some such reactions of anger, indignation, or ridicule may stem from the perception of the movie version as a blunt lie.

This attitude may be explained if we distinguish between axiomatic beliefs and provisionally held propositions concerning given data.[19] Whereas beliefs carry a high truth value for those maintaining them, provisional propositions are held as feasible yet unasserted. Following this distinction, I would like to suggest that viewers angered at some fictions that offer feasible optional accounts of other fictions, may in these cases be holding as important to them a rational, axiomatic belief in the maintenance of the originality of a work. However, while this belief is rational insofar as it relates to works that *pretend* to be the original, it may be the case that such a belief biases their assessment of the optional version, overshadowing and blocking the optional thinking that the latter version engenders. I presume this is the case underlying many critical reactions to the movie version. However, *Alice in Wonderland* does not pretend to be a faithful (or *the* faithful) rendition of the original. In fact, the movie flaunts the fact that it is an optional account of Lewis Carroll's original, for example by its being framed as a sequel where Alice, now older, recalls her seven-year-old fantasies and relives them differently. Hence, in this case, reactions stemming from the belief in originality bias some of these viewers' comprehension of the movie and disengage them from fruitfully assessing and comparing the viable alternative it offers to the original.

This distinction between axiomatic beliefs and provisional propositions goes a long way in explaining many cases where movies' narrative fictions fail to engage some of their viewers, including those films that encourage optional thinking. This is because such movies violate "external" beliefs that some viewers rationally hold as important, beliefs that overshadow their consideration of the feasible nature of the fiction. When a film violates important things we believe in, our mode of interaction with it may shift from our entertaining its illusion as feasible to finding it unacceptable due to its lies.

4.2.2.4. Movies with Narrative Alternatives to History: *Inglourious Basterds*

The distinction between beliefs and (fictional) propositions is particularly relevant to fictional movies that recreate historical trajectories but include counterfactual elements. In such cases, some viewers who know the history recounted rationally hold the belief that the events depicted occurred differently and if such events are important for such viewers, they will perceive the historical inaccuracy as a blunt lie. Many Jews, for example, have condemned Roberto Benigni's *Life is Beautiful* (1997). They consider the movie's depiction of how a father manages to divert his son's attention away from the Nazi extermination of Jews in the camp they are in, by framing the occurrences as part of a game, to be counterfactual and utterly improbable. This improbability is taken to result in a lightening of the gravity of Nazi crimes and consequently as a desecration of the memory of the murdered Jews.[20] For these viewers, Benigni's fictional account, in its violation of a truth they rationally hold as important to them, is condemnable. Many other Jews, however, have found the movie diverting and moving because they consider its counterfactual aspect to be flaunted precisely because of its game-likeness, whereas in all other respects the movie was not counterfactual, hinting at, and at times powerfully evoking the horror of the holocaust.

In any case, Benigni's film does not encourage optional thinking because its counterfactual aspect is not viable as an alternative option in that it does not imply that things could have been different. I suggest that popular movies that offer virtual histories that do not suggest feasible alternative futures to the accepted-as-known past do not seem to evoke optional thinking. This is because outlining a suspenseful story that suggests a single, imaginary trajectory that neatly fits into accepted historical evidence does not imply historical viable optionality in the sense that things could have turned out differently. It rather offers a looped optionality constrained by evidence accepted as factual. Many historical films, such as *Hitler: The Downfall* (Oliver Hirschbiegel 2004), while outlining a peculiar, suspenseful, historical conjecture, do not encourage optional thinking. Admittedly, while *Hitler: The Downfall*, in its fictional conjecture about Hitler's last days in the bunker, offers a fresh outlook on established perceptions of the murderous tyrant, I contend that viewers perceive this (emotionally powerful) conjecture as a recursive and structurally closed variation played out among well known facts.

I would like to suggest that historical dramas may powerfully encourage optional thinking if they include viable counterfactuals that, to quote Ferguson, stem from "those alternatives which we can show on the basis of contemporary evidence that contemporaries actually considered" (Ferguson 1999: 86). Unlike films like *Life is Beautiful* or *Hitler: The Downfall*, such films imply for viewers that history could have feasibly taken another course, encouraging not just optional thinking but also the notion of an ultimate unpredictability in the course of past events, gearing viewers toward considering viable and optional futures.

Given the discussion of the violation of viewers' beliefs by counterfactuals and the attendant blocking of optional thinking, I would like to further suggest that counterfactuals need to be admitted and flaunted as such, thus avoiding their being perceived as fakes. In such cases, it is precisely the feasible, flaunted lie that powerfully encourages optional thinking, by highlighting the fact that history could have taken a different course if the counterfactual yet feasible historical trajectory had occurred.[21]

An exemplary and to my knowledge unique example of this strategy can be found in Quentin Tarantino's virtual history movie about the Second World War, *Inglourious Basterds*.[22] This revenge-narrative movie, set in Nazi-occupied France during World War II, tells of a group of Jewish-United States soldiers (the "Basterds") chosen by Lt. Aldo Raine (Brad Pitt) to brutally kill and scalp as many Nazis as possible so as to spread terror among the Nazi army and its command ranks. This revenge trajectory parallels a second one in which the Jewish young woman Shosanna Dreyfus (Melanie Laurent), after escaping the slaughter of her family by the diabolical Nazi Colonel Hans Landa (Christoph Waltz), plots to take revenge upon Landa, Hitler, Goebbels, and other central figures of the Third Reich high command. She plots to avenge herself during the premiere screening of a Nazi propaganda movie at a theater she runs, which is to be attended by Hitler and other leaders of the Nazi regime. These two revenge tracks start to converge when the British are informed of the Nazi leaders' attendance at the screening. They send Lieutenant Archie Hicox (Michael Fassbender) to occupied France where he joins the "Basterds" and double agent Bridget von Hammersmark (Diane Kruger) in a tavern. A Gestapo officer exposes them upon noticing Hicox's foreign accent and his non-German signaling when ordering drinks. After what Raine terms from outside the tavern a "Mexican standoff," a shootout ensues leaving everybody in the tavern dead except for Hammersmark (she is later strangled by Landa after he exposes her by fitting a shoe that she left in the tavern to her foot). Raine and the remaining two "Basterds," Donny (Eli Roth) and Omar (Omar Doom), posing as Italians, arrive at the theater. They are caught by Landa, who later releases them and lets them into the screening after striking a deal with the United States authorities to receive shelter. The movie climaxes when the two revenge trajectories converge during the screening. Although Shosanna does not get to witness her revenge because she is shot dead, her lover carries out her plan by blocking all exits from the theater and igniting nitrate film stock that sets the theater on fire. On the burning screen Shosanna's image appears telling the audience they are about to be killed by a Jew. The "Basterds," seated at the screening, complement the fire with their own shooting down of the Nazi dignitaries, notably Hitler, Goebbels, and Borman, thereby "shaking the very annals of history," as one commentator put it.[23] The film ends with Raine carving a swastika on Landa's forehead which he describes as his "masterpiece."

Tarantino's suspenseful and diverting movie is based upon factual history in that Goebbels and Hitler loved movies, there was a plot to assassinate Hitler, sentiments of revenge ran high amongst Jews, Nazi murderous sadism is well documented, double agents and infiltrations into occupied France were abundant, there was partisan Jewish resistance, several Nazi officers reached agreements with the United States authorities and saved their lives, etc. In all these respects Tarantino's movie is a regular, action-packed, suspenseful war movie. Had the revenge plots failed, *Inglourious Basterds* might have offered another feasible yet historically loopy conjecture about a commando revenge unit. What makes this movie a powerfully stimulant for optional thinking amongst viewers is its surprising counterfactual ending, whereby the revenge plots succeed and the Third Reich high command is shot and burned to death. This counterfactual ending, feasible within the movie's internal probabilities, compels viewers to reassess it against their knowledge of the historical trajectory. Tarantino also avoids rational rejections of its counterfactual element as faked, because it flaunts its counterfactuality through its abundant intertextual stylistic and thematic references, constantly pointing to the fact that its fiction is primarily borrowed from other movies. Some widely familiar references include: the western genre (the scalping, the "Mexican standoff," the Basterds' nicknames "The Bear Jew" and "Aldo the Apache," the revenge theme, etc.); World War II movies about a select commando unit on a mission, like *Guns of Navarone* (J. Lee Thompson 1961), *Where Eagles Dare* (Brian G. Hutton 1968), or *The Dirty Dozen* (Robert Aldrich 1967); the shoe fitting reference to Cinderella; German expressionist films (through style and the mention of director G.W. Pabst); film noir style and its figure of the femme fatale which is used to portray double agent Bridget von Hammersmark; and so on and so forth.[24] Finally, countering popular movies' use of surprise structures to enhance suspense and block previously suggested options as not true to the fiction,[25] the surprising counterfactual climax of this movie is not, and cannot be, exchanged for the historical fact it strongly recalls. In this manner, *Inglourious Basterds* exploits rather than blocks the optional thinking effect of surprise by compelling viewers to assess its feasible narrative trajectory and counterfactual closure against the historical trajectory known to the (majority of) viewers. This is done in a manner that instills in viewers the notion of the unpredictability of history and the possible futures that could ensue if "those alternatives which we can show on the basis of contemporary evidence that contemporaries actually considered," would have materialized.

The above analysis shows how popular films cue optional thinking without foregoing the grounds that make most movies popular. The movies chosen for analysis represent paradigmatic cases that best exhibit how the strategies that make movies popular can be effectively used to cue optional thinking. These comprehensive paradigmatic cases subsume other movie modalities referenced throughout that may cue optional thinking but seem to do so less effectively. Thus *Sliding Doors* subsumes some "time travel" movies that incorporate alternate trajectories within the fiction and cue optional thinking; *Rashomon* subsumes some "unreliable narrator" movies; *Alice in Wonderland* subsumes some film remakes or sequels; and *Inglourious Basterds* subsumes some mockumentaries. In the following concluding chapter, after a summary rendition of the argument made throughout this study, I will consider other films' modalities and strategies that may encourage optional thinking and are not subsumed under the paradigmatic cases analysed.

Notes

1. By "indexing" Carroll means the drawing of the viewer's attention to something important in the story, as in a close up showing the spectator that the villain has secretly drawn a gun (why is he doing this?); by "scaling" he means the changing of the relations between objects, as when the camera moves away to reveal the villain standing behind the sheriff (will he shoot the sheriff from behind?); and by "bracketing" Carroll means the insertion of material taken from another context, as when you insert the sound of an off-screen gunshot that kills the villain (who killed him?). In such a manner, films also frame the answers to the questions raised, as when a consequent shot answers the question, "Who killed the villain?" by showing up close the sheriff's beloved wife holding a smoking gun, followed by a zoom-out rescaling to reveal her standing on a rooftop overlooking the scene.

2. See the analysis of Spielberg's *Duel* (1971) in chapter 2 of this volume, showing how such reduction entails an ongoing narrative and audiovisual effort to block overlooming options other than whether the protagonist will survive the attack of the menacing truck driver.

3. On mind wandering see, for example, Mason et al. (2007: 393–395). I do not claim that all cognitive performance is effortless or that our capacity for cognitive tasks that require attention is unlimited. I also concur with the proposition that high emotional arousal narrows our attention capacity (Kahneman 1973). I simply claim here that the narrative reduction offered by movies encouraging closed mindedness far from exhausts our capacity for cognitive tasks that require attention as Tan suggests. Movies are not "precision machines" that offer an exact and exhausting tradeoff between mental and emotional effort. Movies that engender a heightened need for closure do narrow our attention but do not exhaust it. The reason viewers seek closure is not because they have exhausted their cognitive attention capacity. What they can "barely meet" is the prolonged uncertainty of suspense.

4. Conversely, vagueness does not necessarily mean that images are complex. This latter notion is implied in Andre Bazin's notion of ambiguity as embedded in his conception of the realist long take: "[D]epth of focus reintroduces ambiguity

into the structure of the image .... The uncertainty in which we find ourselves as to the spiritual key or the interpretation we should put on the film is built into the very design of the image." This does not mean of course that long-take, deep-focused images need to be ambiguous and undecipherable. They can be complex yet clear. This is evidenced, for example, in Orson Welles's *Citizen Kane* (1941), a movie considered by Bazin to be a milestone within the realist cinematic tradition. In this film, Wells deploys deep-focused one-shot sequences, covering an entire dramatic event without recourse to cutting, thereby preserving the event's duration while enhancing spatial depth. An archetypal example of this strategy can be seen in the scene from the film where Kane as a child is being given away by his mother to the guardianship of a financier named Thatcher. The whole scene is conveyed in one long, deep-focused shot in which we see the mother in the foreground discussing the arrangement with Thatcher while in the background, through a window, we see little Kane happily playing in the snow, unaware of the transaction that will change the course of his life forever. Facing this complex shot, the viewer understands in an unambiguous manner what is going on in light of the future consequences as presented prior to this by the movie. While this in itself does not generate optional thinking, this one-shot scene is complex yet clear.

5. Branigan refers to these films as "multiple-draft films" while also addressing some of the concerns shared in this study (Branigan 2002: 105–114).

6. Bordwell and Branigan also discuss Krzysztof Kieslowski's *Blind Chance* (1981), but in it only one destiny is true to the fiction.

7. Bordwell's awareness of the viewers' cognitive comprehension constraints is very much to the point, particularly when pitted against the naïve presumption of postmodernism, including the recent variant that uses complexity theory (e.g., Simons 2008: 111–126). The latter end up heralding arbitrariness as evoking complexity, or value over-complex narrative bifurcations without taking into serious consideration the cognitive constraints of short-term memory and the inability to split attention, as well as the cognitive-emotional motivations for narrative engagement. I think this claim is fundamental for optional-thinking-based movies that address humans rather than computers. In other words, while the calculative power of computers may generate endless forking story possibilities, and while the philosophical, social, or scientific implications of such narrative idea are intriguing, attempts to actually devise such a labyrinth will divert the viewer's attention towards memorizing and frustrating puzzle-solving, cognitive activities. These activities, however, have little to do with the satisfying, deep engagement offered by narrative or with the limitations of viewers' cognitive processing of narrative. They are also needless, since the different intriguing implications of such narrative ideas can be fruitfully explored in a deeply cognitively and emotionally engaging way through the suggestion of their implications by a restricted, contained, cognitively manageable, optional-thinking-based narrative film construction.

8. Arbitrary interrelations between narrative threads will most probably lead the viewer to lose sight of, or interest in whatever went on before or after the transition, engendering thereby viewer distraction. This will probably happen

even if each narrative thread is cohering within its own trajectory and even if transitions are signposted. This is because radical narrative shifts to unrelated stories would probably frustrate the viewer's striving for coherence, triggered by the mere fact that these narrative threads are held together in the same movie.

9. Richard Gerrig has suggested that, based on an evolutionary survival need to generate flexible responses to effectively deal with unexpected events, we have developed an automated cognitive response based on an expectation of uniqueness "incorporated within the cognitive processes that guide the expectations of narratives ...[, given] that our moment-by-moment processes evolve in response to the brute fact of nonrepetition" (Gerrig 1993: 170–171). While the aim of this suggestion is to try and explain away how recidivist readers are in suspense upon a second reading, a notion justifiably rejected by Carroll, it is relevant for the case discussed above (N. Carroll 1996b: 89).

10. This does not mean that viewers can follow any number of options, or even more than three or four, due to cognitive load limitations. The important issue, however, is not how many options can be viably entertained by viewers but the fact that viewers can entertain as viable two or three such options. This is enough to evoke the notion of optionality in viewers.

11. Using unreliable narrators could be a powerful strategy to encourage optional thinking, given that the viewer is compelled to reconstruct an optional story out of the biased or misleading version of the narrator. However, most movies using this strategy revolve around the impossibility to reach the truth (e.g., *eXistenZ*, *Mulholland Drive*), thus encouraging loopy thinking, or render the unreliable narrator's option as false rather than possible or probable within the fictional world, thus encouraging closed mindedness (e.g., *The Sixth Sense*).

12. This viewer effect can be traced in the somewhat far-fetched symbolism attributed to *Rashomon* by some commentators, whereby the film somehow symbolizes Japan's existential disarray and moral decay after its defeat in World War II (e.g., Davidson 1987: 159–166). As will be shown, such an interpretation and looped thought cannot be comprehensibly attributed to the movie and its overall experience by most viewers.

13. There is an earlier flashback recounted by the woodcutter to the commoner and describing how he found the dead body. This flashback, while not in court, is also introduced by the woodcutter facing the camera. I would like to point out that while the focus of my analysis leads me to downplay the simple stylistic virtuosity of the movie, it is worth mentioning that this flashback starts with a long sequence showing the woodcutter entering deeper and deeper into the forest. The sequence is deployed through alternating panning or tracking shots of him from different directions, angles, and distances, conveying a strong sense of suspenseful forward movement that, notwithstanding other symbolism, sets in motion the suspenseful trajectory of the movie.

14. On how perspective taking engenders empathy for characters, see section 2.2.3. above.

15. Formalism and structuralism offered an important precedent for this notion, in claiming respectively that the value of component units within a work of art (formalism) or a structure (structuralism) resides more in their internal

interrelations than in their relation to components from without the work of art or structure. However, these approaches lack attention to the force and dynamics of the narrative succession in determining this interrelation.

16. While this external knowledge "should" not be part of our imaginative response to the story, it often is. In such cases, that is, when viewers do consciously consider information external to the fiction to be pertinent, their attention is divided between the evolving narrative at hand and the sporadic recall of external references.

17. This is dependent of course upon acquaintance with the originating text such as the acquaintance with Shakespeare's *Hamlet* by many viewers when watching Kenneth Branagh's adaptation (1996). Otherwise, such movies offer a nonoptional narrative trajectory. While I focus here upon adaptations of books to films, the claims made are as relevant, under the same conditions, to many film remakes, such as Branagh's *Hamlet* when considered as a remake of Lawrence Olivier's movie *Hamlet* (1948), or *Point of No Return* (John Badham 1993), the United States remake of the French movie *Nikita* (Luc Besson 1990).

18. A typical critical response to the movie can be found in Amy Biancolli's review (tagged as "top critic" by Rotten Tomatoes website) that was published in the *Houston Chronicle* on March 4, 2010. She writes,

    Alice in Wonderland? Is that what it is? Because it doesn't look like any Alice I know. It has action scenes, traumatic flashbacks, heartfelt bonding between Alice and the Mad Hatter whose gimongous green eyes swell with emotion. There's even a scene where Alice gets hit on by the Knave of Hearts, one of the skeevier conceits in this fumbled Disney update. But its single biggest failing—an affront to Lewis Carroll and the charms of nonsense literature—is the fact that it makes sense. Director Tim Burton and screenwriter Linda Woolverton have labored hard to shoehorn the arch, asymmetrical balderdash of the original works (both *Alice's Adventures in Wonderland* and *Through the Looking-Glass*) into a 3–D, CG-enhanced extravaganza of boring and time-worn fantasy conventions. It isn't often a 3–D movie almost puts me to sleep.

19. See Ben Shaul (1997: 4–5). Noel Carroll has suggested a similar distinction between believing something to be true and imagining it as feasible (Carroll 1996b). Carroll's distinction was phrased as a counter argument-against film theories that presume that viewers get emotional about what is presented before them because they are manipulated into holding the irrational belief that what they see is real. Rejecting the notion of viewers' irrationality, he suggested that we can get emotional in reaction to fictions that we know are not true, suggesting that while both types of propositions can induce emotions, fictional stories are imaginary feasible accounts that do not require that we irrationally believe in them for us to get emotional about them.

20. Someone even wrote a book about it (Niv 2003).

21. I am not contending here that the creator of a fiction lies. I contend that he/she may, deliberately or not, insinuate for viewers who may judge the fiction in terms of truths and lies that a counterfactual event actually occurred, and

I discuss the ramifications of this. That is, I think a creator of fiction should be aware of when it may be implied (for some viewers) that an important counterfactual element of the story actually happened, and consider the ramifications.

22. Other counterfactual history films include mockumentaries that construe counterfactual histories, such *AFR* (Morten Hartz Kaplers 2007), which portrays the counterfactual assassination of the Danish Prime Minister Anders Fogh Rasmussen; or *Death of a President* (Gabriel Range 2006), about the fictional assassination of George W. Bush, in 2007 in Chicago. Other movies that illustrate this process include *The Family Man* (Bret Rattner 2000), *Back to the Future* (Robert Zemeckis 1985), *A Christmas Carol* (Brian Desmond Hurst 1951), and *It's a Wonderful Life* (Frank Capra 1946). In the latter film, George Bailey (James Stewart) is shown by an angel what the world he knows would have been like if he had never been born. In the film, the world Bailey sees appears as real as the one he knows, and in it he is shown how his brother Harry, who was a war hero in the "real" world of the film, could have drowned in a skating accident at the age of eight because Bailey was not there to save him as he did, since in the counterfactual world Bailey was not born. As Rubin puts it, in these counterfactual films "the causal effects of actions involves the comparison of potential outcomes, which are the stream of events at the same times but after different actions" (Rubin 2007: 71).

23. The comment was written by "The Massie Twins" for the Internet Movie Database (IMDB). See <http://www.imdb.com/title/tt0361748/plotsummary> (accessed Oct. 20, 2010).

24. For lists of references in this film see: <http://www.suite101.com/content/the-cinephiles-guide-to-inglourious-basterds-a147275>; <http://www.filmspotting.net/forum/index.php?topic=6410.0>; <http://www.tarantino.info/wiki/index.php/Inglourious_Basterds_movie_references_guide> (accessed Oct. 20, 2010).

25. Surprise, in and of itself, triggers optional thinking in order to try and explain the discrepancy caused by it. While initially this explanatory process is conducted according to readily available schemes, failure to do so may engender optional hypotheses and knowledge revisions. However, as discussed above (e.g., in relation to *Silence of the Lambs* or *The Sixth Sense*) incorporating surprise within a suspense structure blocks optional thinking.

5

Conclusion

"Optional thinking" refers to our cognitive ability to assess or to generate diverging, converging, or competing sequences of optional reasons for, consequences of, or solutions to different life problems. This study has shown that while narratives are inherently optional given the probabilistic nature of their causality, most narrative films do not encourage optional thinking. Most popular movies discourage optional thinking and encourage closed mindedness in viewers. This is because the different strategies that make these movies popular, such as the deployment of narrative suspense or surprise, in conjunction with the viewer's empathy for the protagonist, heighten the viewer's need to avoid distressing uncertainty by seeking resolution and closure. This heightened need, inclining viewers to constrain their optional thinking, is then gratifyingly reciprocated by a gradual reduction of the narrative to a single trajectory and closure that seems to strictly and necessarily ensue from what went on, thereby blocking optional thinking in viewers.

However, it was also shown that most narrative films that disrupt the coherence of the narrative or dismantle suspense, surprise, and the viewer's empathy for characters probably generate confusion, split attention, or distraction. While these strategies may engender occasional mental rumination, streams of associations, or vague, localized optional thinking, they fail to encourage optional thinking in terms of causes and consequences that are meaningfully alternative to other such trajectories.

As argued, this does not mean that popular movies cannot encourage optional thinking in viewers. This study has suggested under what terms popular movies may encourage optional thinking without foregoing the characteristics that make them popular. For movies to evoke viable optional thinking, alternative options that indicate feasible alternative futures (rather than looped variations) must carry enough information to be construed by viewers as alternative narrative tracks or perspectives in a manner that compels viewers to compare and assess the alternatives for comprehension. Given the cognitive tendency and capacity of viewers to entertain (up to a point) more than one narrative track or perspective, strategies of suspense, surprise, and empathy for characters do not reduce but can rather enhance, under fear of incomprehension, the viewers' attention to these alternatives. I have shown how this might occur in movies that compel viewers to assess and compare viable alternative narrative tracks materialized within the fictional illusion (e.g., *Run Lola Run*). I have also shown how some movie adaptations may evoke optional thinking in those viewers well acquainted with the external referenced narrative, whether fictional (e.g., *Alice in Wonderland*) or historical (e.g., *Inglourious Basterds*). Finally, I instantiated how this process might occur in movies that encourage the viewer's empathy with different protagonists who hold diverging perspectives on shared events or on each other (e.g., *Rashomon*).

This does not mean that only such films may encourage optional thinking in viewers. It does mean, however, that the narrative and affective structure of such films answer to most relevant suggested conditions under which movies may be taken to encourage optional thinking. This is irrespective, of course, of cases where viewers lose track for various subjective reasons, or when the film fails to engage the viewers' imagination in its fictional illusion for reasons of incompetence. Such situations apply, however, to any movie, be it optional or not.

More interesting in respect of subjective viewer responses are those cases where the movie fails because it violates beliefs viewers hold to be important, a process that dismantles the movies' intended affective structure, exchanging it for an emotional response based upon indignation or ridicule of the movie. This latter attitude can even extend to the whole film, thus apparently engendering optional thinking in the sense that the violated belief proposes a viable alternative external to the fiction that, while comprehending all the alternatives internal to the fiction, takes these to be looped variations irrespective of whether they imply alternative futures within the fiction. In such cases the viewer implies something like, "I can see what was intended but I do not buy it." This process has been well described by Stuart Hall. Premising that messages encoded in a text are relevantly decoded by recipients, Hall suggests nevertheless that the "encoding/decoding" process need not be univocal or complementary in that "it is possible for a viewer perfectly to understand both the literal and the connotative inflection given by a discourse but to decode the message in a globally contrary way. He/she detotalizes the message in the preferred code in order to retotalize the message within some alternative framework of reference" (Hall 1980: 138). I contend, however, that in such cases where a viably structured movie that induces optional thinking is taken by some viewers to be looped for reasons that reside outside its fictional illusion, viable optional thinking is blocked for these viewers. This is due to their imposition upon the movie of a loop that is external to the fiction. For such viewers the illusion fails along with the viable optional-thinking process it does engender for those lending their imagination to the fictional illusion.

5.1. Further Research

The suggested conditions set up for movies to evoke viable optional thinking do not necessarily exclude cases where movies that are not compatible with these conditions might engender optional thinking in some viewers. I contend, however, that if the viewer is affectively and cognitively engaged as intended by such nonoptional movies (i.e., most movies) it is more difficult for this to occur. I would like to briefly consider, however, some such potential options that call for further research.

5.1.1. Conflated Optionality

As already discussed, a potentially fruitful model for optional thinking stemming from postmodern thought was suggested by Doty. He argued that movies may offer viable, different, simultaneously present perspectives and comprehensions that extend throughout a film's cohering narrative trajectory and single closure (Doty 1998). In fact, what Doty's model suggests is that a narrative trajectory can clearly and consistently conflate together two or more optional meanings that extend throughout the movie up to its closure. This proposition is pertinent in respect of Neshat's photograph discussed above in the previous chapter, where two options are conflated into a single photograph that leads the viewer to maintain simultaneously or to shift between two interpretations (i.e., that the woman kisses of her free will a finger placed on her lips, and is simultaneously oppressively silenced by this finger). However, while a movie may do that (and it could, given its inherent optionality), I doubt that this conflation can be meaningfully discerned by a viewer throughout an entire movie with a single trajectory and closure. Doty has instantiated how this might work in his brilliant analysis of *The Women* (George Cukor 1939) by tracing the possible alternative interpretations of the same movie that may be given by viewers with different gender or sexual orientations. However, I contend that while one viewer may interpret the entire movie in one way and another in a different way, it would be very difficult for the same viewer to discern in a consistent and comprehensive manner two or more conflated interpretations simultaneously. This is particularly the case with movies whose aforementioned strategies gear a viewer toward reducing the narrative to a univocal meaning.[1] Indeed, Doty does not seem to suggest this to be the case. While such a strategy is common to retrospective discussions of movies by viewers, and is characteristic of the practice of film research which often detects and construes viable optional interpretations to a movie, viewers can hardly do that when engaged in the fictional illusion of most popular movies. This is not to say that movies do not conflate alternatives. Many movies do, and are even prone to do so given their embedded optionality. I would argue, however, that in such cases (of which there are many), the viewer will construe this as a vague ambiguity rather than weed out each option as an alternative trajectory for the character or for the movie to take. While most movies end up resolving such ambiguity upon closure, some movies even maintain this ambiguity all the way up to their closure. This can be evidenced, for example, in David Cronenberg's *A History of Violence* (2005), where we are left undecided throughout the movie and after the lights go on about the "true" nature of the born-again killer, who is also a devoted family man. This sense of ambiguous irresolution, however, does not translate for viewers into optional trajectories, but rather revolves around the ambiguous nature of humans or of reality. In fact, ambiguous movies that avoid resolution encourage loopy thinking rather than optional thinking, given that the terms of the conflated options close in upon themselves upon closure. Such a response to conflated options characterizes many movies that offer ambiguous characters or ambiguous situations (e.g., Joel and Ethan Cohen's 2009 movie *A Serious Man*).

5.1.2. Divergent Stylistic and Narrative Systems

As already mentioned, a viable model for cueing optional thinking, which stems from formalist thought, consists of an alternation between a stylistic system that carries a predetermined ambiance and accumulated meaning (as in generic styles, such as those of musicals or westerns, with their respective "life is music" or "civilization vs. nature" notions) and a narrative (illusion) with a subject matter and locale that do not pertain to the stylistic system mentioned. In this model, the viewer faces two different semantic systems that s/he can compare.[2] Under such circumstances, and only if these two semantic systems are interrelated so that the viewer needs to consider both as viable alternatives to the developing narrative, such films may engender optional thinking.[3] This can be partly evidenced in Tarantino's use of the western genre in *Inglourious Basterds*, or in Lars von Trier's contradictory use of the musical genre in *Dancer in the Dark*. Thus, while *Inglourious Basterds* is, overall, a Second World War movie set in occupied France, it includes many stylistic, visual, and thematic references to the western genre, which are usually set in the American West in the second half of the nineteenth century. These references include scalping, nicknames such as "The Bear Jew" and "Aldo the Apache"; a "Mexican standoff" and ensuing shootout in a "saloon" (translocated to a German tavern); and a revenge theme in a barn (in rural France). Likewise, Von Trier's movie fashions several scenes within his otherwise bleak and dead-end tragedy as musical numbers, referencing the genre of musicals. For example, the heroine, having heard she is going blind, rides a train, but slowly her ride turns into a rhythmical song and dance piece whose ambiance references the optimism and celebration of life characterized by musicals. Stylistic references such as these introduce the ambiance and semantic meanings accumulated by the respective genres referenced. However, in both films, such references fail to create a viable optional trajectory. Thus, recalling Indians from westerns in the Jews' nicknames in *Inglourious Basterds* may evoke a variety of localized optional thoughts due to the surprising and discrepant juxtaposition (e.g., Jews as nomads may be seen as noble savages: indigenous, wild, in touch with nature and trustworthy, rather than say, their anti-Semitic portrayal as treacherous, greedy, debased, and rootless; or, Jews were not slaughtered like lambs due to their submissive nature). However, these occasional optional-thinking opportunities do not add up in the viewer's mind to a comprehensive narrative trajectory that is a viable alternative to the dominant version suggested by the movie. Moreover, the fact that *Inglourious Basterds* incorporates a variety of other references to many other movie styles (e.g., film noir) cancels out whatever option might have been forming in the viewer's mind, rendering these references as playful quotes whose major function is to indicate that the movie refers to the movie world. Likewise, while the portrayal of the dance in *Dancer in the Dark* may evoke the localized option that optimism may reign in the darkest of places, this does not come about as a viable alternative to the story but rather serves to enhance the added misery gained from being optimistic for a moment.

I would not rule out, however, the option that a stylistic system may engender a viable option for some viewers that are experts on the genre referenced. Such could be the case when cues pointing to the genre allow the expert viewer to construe them into a viable alternative trajectory. Usually, however, such expertise detracts from the emotional engagement with the narrative illusion, encouraging instead a gaming attitude toward the movie. Otherwise, as is usually the case, such cues may only arouse localized, nonviable alternatives to the narrative at hand.

5.1.3. Discontinued Narrative Trajectories

I would like to briefly suggest for further research a strategy that has not been developed to my knowledge but that carries some promise in respect of optional thinking. It came to my mind after discussing with a friend Tarantino's *Inglourious Basterds*. This friend told me that it was interesting for him to see how Tarantino introduced the character of the British agent, who was sent to France and then vanished from the movie with no trace. My friend commented that this led him to ponder about the many people in World War II whose tracks were forever lost and may have used the opportunity to shed their past identity and forge a new one. While my friend's hypothesis was based on his not identifying the British agent in the tavern, his mistaken hypothesis opens up a possibility to engender viable optional thinking through deliberately poor structures that fissure the narrative. Thus, inserting evocative, unresolved narrative tracks that tease viewers to entertain possible feasible outcomes that never materialize, but that if materialized would have affected the overall narrative outcome in alternative ways, may evoke viable optional thinking. I would add, however, that such fissuring may be viable if it refrains from opening up the film to whatever comes to mind, but rather contains such overspill by calculating this fissure so that it operates within the fictional horizon of the movie's overall narrative trajectory and closure.

5.1.4. Evocations of the Viewer's Will to Intervene

Another possible strategy in need of further research concerns the evocation of viable optional thinking by constructing suspenseful situations that encourage the viewer to want to intervene in the narrative. These include situations when characters who arouse the viewer's empathy are unaware of detrimental or positive information the viewer has, or when such characters themselves exhibit a lack of optional thinking due, for example, to their feeling a heightened need for closure. This rare evocation can be found in localized sequences within different movies but it usually encourages the viewer's heightened need for closure due to helplessness. However, arousing localized optional thinking may evince viable optional thinking if the potential horizon of outcomes is contained and the viewer's entertained "what if?" propositions are given extended consideration throughout the movie.

I think these two last potential yet underplayed strategies could be developed in a manner that promises the evocation of viable optional thinking. This, however, remains to be seen.

Notes

1. This explains the ease with which movies surprise us, but it may also explain why viewers sometimes do not comprehend the movie, the reason being their decoding it in a manner that is not supported by the overall narrative trajectory.
2. I am not referring here to a common divergence between style and content characterizing many war or science fiction films, where the narrative trajectory suggests that wars or new technology are bad for humanity, and yet their

spectacular aspect references a discourse on war as the ultimate human challenge, as in Kathryn Bigelow's 2008 movie *The Hurt Locker*, or of new technology as leading to the superseding of human constraints as in *The Matrix*. Such cases fall into the ambiguity trap discussed above.

3. This discussion also pertains to a divergence between a star's established persona's accumulated semantic meaning and its figuring in an opposing or different role within a specific movie, as in Ivan Reitman's 1994 movie *Junior*, where muscle man Arnold Schwarzenegger is pregnant and about to have a baby.

Filmography

2 ou 3 choses que je sais d'elle [Two or Three Things I Know About
   Her] (Jean Luc Godard 1967)
2001: A Space Odyssey (Stanley Kubrick 1968)
A Christmas Carol (Brian Desmond Hurst 1951)
A History of Violence (David Cronenberg 2005)
A Million Dollar Baby (Clint Eastwood 2004)
A Serious Man (Joel and Ethan Cohen 2009)
Adaptation (Spike Jonze/Charlie Kaufman 2002)
AFR (Morten Hartz Kaplers 2007)
Alice in Wonderland (Tim Burton 2010)
All that Jazz (Bob Fosse 1979)
Austin Powers, the Spy Who Shagged Me (Jay Roach 1999)
Back to the Future (Robert Zemeckis 1985)
Battleship Potemkin (Sergei Eisenstein 1925)
Being John Malkovich (Spike Jonze/Charlie Kaufman 1999)
Belle de Jour (Luis Buñuel 1967)
Black or White video clip (John Landis 1991)
Blade Runner (Ridley Scott's director's-cut version of 1982)
Blind Chance (Krzysztof Kieslowski 1981)
Citizen Kane (Orson Welles 1941)
Cronaca di un Amore [Story of a Love Affair] (Michelangelo
   Antonioni 1950)
Dancer in the Dark (Lars von Trier 2000)
Death by Hanging (Nagisa Oshima 1968)
Death of a President (Gabriel Range 2006)
Dr. No (Terence Young 1962)

Duel (Steven Spielberg 1971)
Eich Hefsakti Lefached ve'lamadeti le'ehov et Arik Sharon [How
   I Learned to Overcome My Fear and Came to Love Arik
   Sharon] (Avi Mugrabi 1997)
eXistenZ (David Cronenberg 1999)
Fight Club (David Fincher 1999)
Frenzy (Alfred Hitchcock 1972)
Goldeneye (Martin Campbell 1995)
Goldfinger (Guy Hamilton 1964)
Guns of Navarone (J. Lee Thompson 1961)
Hamlet (Lawrence Olivier 1948)
Hamlet (Kenneth Branagh 1996)
Harry Brown (Daniel Barber 2009)
High Noon (Fred Zinnemann 1952)
Hitler: The Downfall (Oliver Hirschbiegel 2004)
Inception (Christopher Nolan 2010)
Inglourious Basterds (Quentin Tarantino 2009)
It's a Wonderful Life (Frank Capra 1946)
Junior (Ivan Reitman's 1994)
La Chinoise (Jean Luc Godard 1967)
Last Year at Marienbad (Alain Resnais 1961)
Life is Beautiful (Roberto Benigni 1997)
Lost Highway (David Lynch 1997)
Made in USA (Jean Luc Godard 1966)
Masculine/Feminine (Jean Luc Godard 1966)
Memento (Christopher Nolan 2000)
Mulholland Drive (David Lynch 2001)
Nikita (Luc Besson 1990)
No Way Out (Roger Donaldson 1987)
Planet of the Apes (Franklin J. Schaffner 1968)
Point of no Return (John Badham 1993)
Psycho (Alfred Hitchcock 1960)
Pulp Fiction (Quentin Tarantino 1994)
Rashomon (Akira Kurosawa 1950)
Rear Window (Alfred Hitchcock 1954)
Rosemary's Baby (Roman Polanski 1968)

Run Lola Run (Tom Twykers 1998)

Shutter Island (Martin Scorsese 2010)

Silence of the Lambs (Jonathan Demme 1991)

Sixth Sense, The (M. Night Shyamalan 1999)

Sleeper (Woody Allen 1973)

Sliding Doors (Peter Howitt 1998)

The Cabinet of Dr. Caligari (Robert Wiene 1920)

The Dirty Dozen (Robert Aldrich 1967)

The Battle of Elderbush Gulch (D.W. Griffith 1913)

The Family Man (Bret Rattner 2000)

The Ghost Writer (Roman Polanski 2010)

The Hurt Locker (Kathryn Bigelow 2008)

The Man With a Movie Camera (Dziga Vertov 1929)

The Matrix (Andy and Larry Wachowski 1999)

The Mother (Vsevolod Pudovkin 1926)

The Others (Alejandro Amenabar 2001)

The Usual Suspects (Bryan Singer 1995)

The Women (George Cukor 1939)

Timecode (Mike Figgis 2000)

Wavelength (Michael Snow 1967)

Week End (Jean-Luc Godard 1968)

Where Eagles Dare (Brian G. Hutton 1968)

Bibliography

Adorno, T. W. 1997. *Aesthetic Theory*, trans. R. Hullot-Kentor. Minneapolis: University of Minnesota Press.

Althusser, L. 1971a. "Ideology and Ideological State Apparatuses." In *Lenin and Philosophy, and Other Essays*, trans. B. Brewster. London: New Left Books (127–86).

———. 1971b. "Letter on Art in Reply to André Daspre." In *Lenin and Philosophy, and Other Essays*, trans. B. Brewster. London: New Left Books (pp. 221–27).

———. 1971c. "Freud and Lacan (*January 1964, corrected February 1969*). In *Lenin and Philosophy, and Other Essays*, trans. B. Brewster. London: New Left Books (189–219).

Arnheim, R. 1957. *Film as Art*. Berkeley: University of California Press.

———. 1967. *Art and Visual Perception*. Berkeley: University of California Press.

Baars, B. J. 1981. "Cognitive Versus Inference." *American Psychologist* 36 (February): 223–224.

Balazs, B. 1970. *Theory of the Film: Character and Growth of a New Art*. New York: Dover Publications.

Barratt, D. 2009. "'Twist Blindness': The Role of Primacy, Priming, Schemas and Reconstructive Memory in a First-Time Viewing of *The Sixth Sense*." In *Puzzle Films*, ed. W. Buckland. Chichester: Wiley-Blackwell (62–87).

Bar-Tal, D., and Y. Teichman. 2005. *Stereotypes and Prejudice in Conflict: Representations of Arabs in Israeli Jewish Society*. Cambridge: Cambridge University Press.

Barthes, R. 1977. *Image, Music, Text*, trans. S. Heath. New York: Hill and Wang.

Baudrillard, J. 1981. *For a Critique of the Political Economy of the Sign*. St. Louis: Telos.

———. 1995a. *Simulacra and Simulation (The Body in Theory: Histories of Cultural Materialism)*. Michigan: University of Michigan Press.

———. 1995b. *The Gulf War Did Not Take Place*. Bloomington: Indiana University Press.

Baudry, J. L. 1985. "Ideological Effects of the Basic Cinematographic Apparatus." In *Movies and Methods Volume II*, ed. B. Nichols. Berkeley: University of California Press (531–42).

Bazin, A. 1967a. "The Ontology of the Photographic Image." In *What is Cinema? Volume 1*. Berkeley: University of California Press (9–16).

———. 1967b. "The Evolution of the Language of Cinema." In *What is Cinema? Volume 1*. Berkeley: University of California Press (23–40).

Beck, A. T., G. Emery, and R. L. Greenberg. 1985. *Anxiety Disorders and Phobias: A Cognitive Perspective*. New York: Basic Books.

Benard, B. 1991. *Fostering Resiliency in Kids: Protective Factors in the Family, School, and Community*. Portland: Western Center for Drug-Free Schools and Communities.

Benjamin, W. 1969. "The Work of Art in the Age of Mechanical Reproduction." In *Illuminations*, ed. H. Arendt. New York: Schocken Books (217–52).

Ben-Porath, Z. 1983. "Intertextuality." *Hassifrut* 34, 2. [Hebrew] (170–78).

Ben-Shaul, N. 1997. *Mythical Expressions of Siege in Israeli Films*. Lewiston: The Edwin Mellen Press.

———. 2006. *A Violent World: TV News Images of Middle Eastern Terror and War*. Lanham: Rowman and Littlefield Publishers.

———. 2007. *Film: The Key Concepts*. Oxford: Berg Publishers.

———. 2008. *Hyper-narrative Interactive Cinema: Problems and Solutions*. Amsterdam: Rodopi.

Berlyne, D. E. 1971. *Aesthetics and Psychobiology*. New York: Meredith Corporation.

Bhaba, H. K. 1990. "DissemiNation." In *Nation and Narration*, ed. H. K. Bhaba. London: Routledge and Kegan Paul (291–322).

Bordwell, D. 1985. *Narration in the Fiction Film*. Madison: Wisconsin University Press.

———. 2002. "Film Futures." *SubStance* 31, no. 1: 88–104.

Branigan, E. 1992. *Narrative Comprehension and Film*. London: Routledge.

———. 2002. "Nearly True: Forking Plots, Forking Interpretations. A Response to David Bordwell's Film Futures." *SubStance* 31, no. 1: 105–114.

Brecher, M. 1980. *Decisions In Crisis, Israel, 1967 and 1973*. Berkeley: University of California Press..

Brewer, W. F. 1996. "The Nature of Narrative Suspense and the Problem of Re-reading." In *Suspense: Conceptualizations, Theoretical Analyses, and Empirical Explorations*, eds. P. Vorderer, H. J. Wulff, and M. Friedrichsen. Mahwah: Lawrence Erlbaum Associates (107–128).

Brunette, P. and D. Wills. 1989. *Screen/Play: Derrida and Film Theory*. Princeton: Princeton University Press.

Buchner, A. 1995. "Basic Topics and Approaches to the Study of Complex Problem Solving." In *Complex Problem Solving: The European Perspective*, eds. P. A. Frensch and J. Funke. Hillsdale: Lawrence Erlbaum Associates (27–64).

Buckland, W. 2009. *Puzzle Films*, ed. W. Buckland. Chichester: Wiley-Blackwell.

Burch, N. 1981. *Theory of Film Practice*. Princeton: Princeton University Press.

Burleson, B. R., and S. E. Caplan. 1998. "Cognitive Complexity." In *Communication and Personality: Trait Perspectives*, eds. J. C. McCroskey, J. A. Daly, M. M. Martin, and M. J. Beatty. Cresskill: Hampton Press (233–87).

Burns, M. O. and M. E. Seligman. 1991. "Explanatory Style, Helplessness, and Depression." In *Handbook of Social and Clinical Psychology*, eds. C. R. Snyder and D. R. Forsyths. New York: Pergamon Press (267–74).

Burton, J., R. Horowitz, and H. Abeles. 1999. "Learning in and through the Arts: Curriculum Implications." In *Champions of Change: The Impact of the Arts of Learning*, ed. E. Fiske. Washington: Arts Education Partnership (35–45).

Butler, J. 1990. *Gender Trouble*. New York: Routledge.

Cameron, A. 2008. *Modular Narratives in Contemporary Cinema*. Palgrave Macmillan.

Carroll, L. 2009. *Alice's Adventures in Wonderland and Through the Looking-Glass*. Oxford: Oxford University Press.

Carroll, N. 1985. "The Power of Movies." *Daedalus* 114, no. 4: 79–103.

————. 1988. *Mystifying Movies: Fads and Fallacies in Contemporary Film Theory*. New York: Columbia University Press.

————. 1996a. *Theorizing the Movie Image*. Cambridge: Cambridge University Press.

————. 1996b. "The Paradox of Suspense." In *Suspense: Conceptualizations, Theoretical Analyses, and Empirical Explorations*, eds. P. Vorderer, H. J. Wulff, and M. Friedrichsen. Mahwah: Lawrence Erlbaum Associates (71–92).

————. 2007. "Narrative Closure." *Philosophical Studies* 135, no. 1: 1–15.

Chandler, P. and J. Sweller. 1991. "Cognitive Load Theory and the Format of Instruction." *Cognition and Instruction* 8: 293–332.

Christoff, K., A. M. Gordon, J. Smallwood, R. Smith, and J. W. Schooler. 2009. "Experience Sampling During fMRI Reveals Default Network and Executive System Contributions to Mind Wandering." *Proceedings of the National Academy of Sciences of the United States of America* 106, no. 21: 8719–24.

Davidson, J. F. 1987. "Memory of Defeat in Japan: A Reappraisal of *Rashomon*." In *Rashomon*, ed. D. Richie. New Brunswick: Rutgers University Press (159–66).

Dayan, D. 1976. "The Tutor Code of Classical Cinema." In *Movies and Methods*, ed. B. Nichols. Berkeley: University of California Press (438–54).

Decety, J. and J. Stevens. 2009. "Action Representation and its Role in Social Interaction." In *The Handbook of Imagination and*

Mental Simulation, eds. K. D. Markman, W. M. P. Klein, and J. A. Suhr. New York: Psychology Press (3–20).

Derrida, J. and Ronell, A. 1980. "The Law of Genre." *Critical Inquiry* Vol. 7, no. 1: 55–81.

Doane, M. A. 1982. "Film and the Masquerade: Theorizing the Female Spectator." *Screen* 23, no. 3–4: 74–78.

Dorn, C. M. 1999. *Mind in Art: Cognitive Foundations in Art Education.* Mahwah: Lawrence Erlbaum Associates.

Dörner, D., and A. Wearing. 1995. "Complex Problem Solving: Toward a (Computer-Simulated) Theory." In *Complex Problem Solving: The European Perspective*, eds. P. A. Frensch and J. Funke. Hillsdale: Lawrence Erlbaum Associates (65–99).

Doty, A. 1998. "Queer Theory." In *The Oxford Guide to Film Studies*, eds. J. Hill, P. C. Gibson, R. Dyer, E. A. Kaplan, and P. Willemen. Oxford: Oxford University Press (148–52).

———. 2000. "Queerness, Comedy and *The Women.*" In *Flaming Classics, Queering the Film Cannon.* New York: Routledge (79–104).

Dyer, R. 1986. *Heavenly Bodies: Film Stars and Society.* London: British Film Institute.

D'Zurilla, T. J. and A. M. Nezu. 1982. "Social Problem Solving in Adults." In *Advances in Cognitive-Behavioral Research and Therapy, Vol. 1*, ed. P. C. Kendall. New York: Academic Press (202–74).

Eisenstein, S. M. 1949. "A Dialectic Approach to Film Form." In *Film Form.* New York: HBJ Books (45–63).

Eisner, E. W. 1998. "Does Experience in the Arts Boost Academic Achievement?" *Art Education, 51*(1): 7–15.

Elsaesser, T. 2009. "The Mind-Game Film." In *Puzzle Films*, ed. W. Buckland. Chichester: Wiley-Blackwell (13–41).

Ferguson, N., ed. 1999. *Virtual History: Alternatives and Counterfactuals.* New York: Basic Books.

Foucault, M. 1984. "Truth and Power." In *Foucault Reader*, ed. P. Rabinow. New York: Pantheon Books (51–75).

Galinsky, A. D. and G. Ku. 2004. "The Effects of Perspective Taking on Prejudice: The Moderating Role of Self-Evaluation." *Personality and Social Psychology Bulletin* 30, no. 5: 594–604.

Galinsky, A. D. and G. B. Moskowitz. 2000. "Perspective-Taking: Decreasing Stereotype Expression, Stereotype Accessibility, and In-Group Favoritism." *Journal of Personality and Social Psychology* 78, no. 4: 720.

Gallagher, T. 1995. "Shoot-Out at the Genre Corral: Problems in the 'Evolution' of the Western." In *Film Genre Reader II*, ed. B. K. Grant. Austin: University of Texas Press (246–60).

Garst, J., N. L. Kerr, S. E. Harris, and L. A. Sheppard. 2002. "Satisficing in Hypothesis Generation." *American Journal of Psychology* 115, no. 4: 475–500.

Geahigan, G. 1997. "Art Criticism: From Theory to Practice." In *Art Criticism and Education*, eds. T. Wolff and G. Geahigan. Urbana: University of Illinois Press (125–278).

Gerrig, R. J. 1993. *Experiencing Narrative Worlds: On the Psychological Activities of Reading*. New Haven: Yale University Press.

Gombrich, E. H. 1969. "The Evidence of Images I: The Variability of Vision." In *Interpretation: Theory and Practice*, ed. C. S. Singleton. Baltimore: The John Hopkins Press (35–68).

Gramsci, A. 1971. *Selections from the Prison Notebooks*. London: Lawrence and Wishart.

Grodal, T. 2009. *Embodied Visions: Evolution, Emotions, Culture, and Film*. Oxford: Oxford University Press.

Heath, S. 1981. "Narrative Space." In *Questions of Cinema*. Bloomington: Indiana University Press (19–75).

Husserl, E. 1999. *Cartesian Meditations: An Introduction to Phenomenology*, trans. D. Cairns. Dordrecht: Kluwer Academic Publishers.

Irigaray, L. 1985. *This Sex Which Is Not One*. Ithaca: Cornell University Press.

James, W. 1950. *Principles of Psychology, Vol. 1*. New York: Dover Publications.

Jameson, F. 1991. *Post-modernism, Or, the Cultural Logic of Late Capitalism*. Durham: Duke University Press.

Jones, E., F. Hoffman, L. Moore, G. Ratcliff, S. Tibbits, and B. Click. 1995. *National Assessment of College Student Learning: Identifying College Graduates' Essential Skills in Writing, Speech and Listening, and Critical Thinking.* Washington: National Center for Education Statistics.

Joyce, J. 1990. *Ulysses.* New York: Vintage.

Kahneman, D. 1973. *Attention and Effort.* New Jersey: Englewood Cliffs Inc.

Kahneman, D. and A. Tversky. 2000. *Choice, Values, Frames.* Cambridge: Cambridge University Press.

Kazanskij, B. 1981. "The Nature of Cinema." In *Russian Formalist Film Theory*, ed. H. Eagle. Ann Arbor: Michigan Slavic Publications (101–30).

Kessel, J. 2007. *Belle de Jour*, trans. Judith Thurman. London: Duckworth & Co.

Kinder, M. 2002. "Narrative Equivocations between Movies and Games." In *The New Media Book*, London: BFI (119–32).

Knee, A. 1995. "Generic Change in the Cinema." *Iris* 20: 31–39.

Krauss, R. M. and S. R. Fussell. 1991. "Perspective-Taking in Communication: Representations of Others' Knowledge in Reference." *Social Cognition* 9: 2–24.

Kristeva, J. 1980. *Desire in Language.* New York: Columbia University Press.

Kruglanski, A. W. 1980. "Lay Epistemo-logic Process and Contents: Another Look at Attribution Theory." *Psychological Review* 87, no. 1: 70–87.

———. 1988. "Knowledge as a Social Psychological Construct." In *The Social Psychology of Knowledge*, eds. D. Bar-Tal and A. W. Kruglanski. Cambridge: Cambridge University Press (109–141).

———. 2004. *The Psychology of Closed Mindedness.* New York: Psychology Press.

Kruglanski, A.W., and D. M. Webster. 1996. "Motivated Closing of the Mind: 'Seizing' and 'Freezing.'" *Psychological Review* 103, no. 2: 263–283.

Kuhn, T. S. 1970. *The Structure of Scientific Revolutions.* Chicago: University of Chicago Press.

Lacan, J. 1977. "The Mirror Stage as Formative of the Function of the I." In *Ecrits, a Selection.* New York: W.W. Norton and Company (1–7).

Lamm, C., C. D. Batson, and J. Decety. 2007. "The Neural Basis of Human Empathy: Effects of Perspective-Taking and Cognitive Appraisal." *Journal of Cognitive Neuroscience* 19: 42–58.

Lampert, N. 2006. "Critical Thinking Dispositions as an Outcome of Art Education." *Studies in Art Education* 47, no. 3: 215–28.

Lazarus, R. S. 1984. "On the Primacy of Cognition." *American Psychologist* 39, February: 124–29.

Lévi-Strauss, C. 1963. "The Structural Study of Myth." In *Structural Anthropology*. New York: Basic Books Inc (106–231).

Manovich, L. 2001. *The Language of New Media*. Cambridge: MIT Press.

Margolis, H. 1987. *Patterns, Thinking, and Cognition: A Theory of Judgment*. Chicago: University of Chicago Press.

Mason, M. F., M. I. Norton, J. D. Van Horn, D. M. Wegner, S. T. Grafton, and C. N. Macrae. 2007. "Wandering Minds: The Default Network and Stimulus-Independent Thought." *Science* 315, no. 5810: 393–95.

Mayer, R. E. 1992. *Thinking, Problem Solving, Cognition*. Second edition. New York: W. H. Freeman and Company.

Mayseless, O. and A. W. Kruglanski. 1987. "What Makes You So Sure? Effects of Epistemic Motivations on Judgmental Confidence." *Organizational Behavior and Human Decision Processes* 39: 162–83.

McAuliffe, C., P. Corcoran, P. Hickey, B. C. McLeavey. 2008. "Optional Thinking Ability among Hospital-Treated Deliberate Self-Harm Patients: A 1–Year Follow-up Study." *British Journal of Clinical Psychology* 47, no. 1: 43–58.

McGowan, T. 2011. *Out of Time: Desire in Atemporal Cinema*. University of Minnesota Press.

Mead, G.H. 1934. *Mind, Self and Society*. Chicago: University of Chicago Press.

Menna, R., and N. J. Cohen. 1997. "Social Perspective Taking." In *Psychological Mindedness: A Contemporary Understanding*, eds. M. E. McCallum and W. E. Piper. Munich: Lawrence Erlbaum (189–210).

Metz, C. 1986. *The Imaginary Signifier: Psychoanalysis and the Cinema*. Indiana: Indiana University Press

Meyer,W., M. Niepel, U. Rudolph, and A. Schützwohl. 1992. "An Experimental Analysis of Surprise." *Cognition and Emotion* 5: 295–311.

Michelson, A. 1970. "Film and the Radical Aspiration." In *Film Culture Reader*, ed. P. Adams Sitney. New York: Praeger (404–21).

———. 1979. "About Snow." *October* 8: 111–24.

Mulvey, L. 1985. "Visual Pleasure and Narrative Cinema." in *Movies and Methods Vol. 2*, ed. B. Nichols. Berkeley: University of California Press (303–314).

Neale, S. 1995. "Questions of Genre." In *Film Genre Reader II*, ed. B. K. Grant. Austin: University of Texas Press (159–83).

Newell, A., and H. A. Simon. 1972. *Human Problem Solving*. Englewood Cliffs: Prentice-Hall.

Niv, K. 2003. *Life is Beautiful, But Not for Jews: Another View of the Film by Benigni*. Lanham: Scarecrow Press.

Oswald, P. A. 1996. "The Effects of Cognitive and Affective Perspective Taking on Empathic Concern and Altruistic Helping." *The Journal of Social Psychology* 136, no. 5: 613–23.

Paul, R., L. Elder, and T. Bartell. 1997. *California Teacher Preparation for Instruction in Critical Thinking: Research Findings and Policy Recommendations*. Sacramento: California Commission on Teacher Credentialing.

Perkins, D. 1994. *The Intelligent Eye: Learning to Think by Looking at Art*. Los Angeles: Getty Publications.

Perry, W. 1999. *Forms of Ethical and Intellectual Development in the College Years: A Scheme*. San Francisco: Jossey-Bass Publishers.

Plantinga, C. 2009. *Moving Viewers: American Film and the Spectator's Experience*. Berkeley: University of California Press.

Platt, J. J. and G. Spivack. 1977. *Measures of Interpersonal Problem Solving for Adults and Adolescents*. Hahnemann: Dept. of Mental Health Sciences, Hahnemann Medical College, Philadelphia.

Platt, J. J., G. Spivack, N. Altman, and D. Altman. 1975. "Adolescent Problem-Solving Thinking." *Journal of Consulting and Clinical Psychology* 42: 787–93.

Polkinghorne, D. E. 1988. *Narrative Knowing and the Human Sciences*. Albany: State University of New York Press.

Propp, V. 1968. *Morphology of the Folktale*, ed. L. Wagner. Austin: University of Texas Press.

Rath, J. F., D. M. Langenbahn, D. Simon, R. L. Sherr, J. Fletcher, and L. Diller. 2004. "The Construct of Problem Solving in Higher Level Neuropsychological Assessment and Rehabilitation." *Archives of Clinical Neuropsychology* 19: 613–35.

Rayfield, D. 1997. *Anton Chekhov: A Life*. New York: Henry Holt and Company.

Reisenzein, R., W. U. Meyer, and A. Schützwohl. 1996. "Reactions to Surprising Events: A Paradigm for Emotion Research." In *Proceedings of the 9th Conference of the International Society for Research on Emotions*, ed. N. Frijda. Toronto: ISRE, 292–96.

Richardson, B. 1997. *Unlikely Stories*. London: Associated University Presses.

Ringelband, O. J., C. Misiak, and R. H. Kluwe. 1990. "Mental Models and Strategies in the Control of a Complex System." In *Mental Models and Human–Computer Interaction, Vol. 1*, eds. D. Ackermann and M. J. Tauber. Amsterdam: Elsevier Science Publishers, 151–64.

Rokeach, M. 1968. *Beliefs, Attitudes, and Values*. San Francisco: Jossey-Bass.

Rubin, D. B. 2007. "Statistical Inference for Causal Effects, with Emphasis on Applications on Psychometrics and Education." In *Handbook of Statistics, Volume 26: Psychometrics*, eds. C. R. Rao and S. Sinharay. Amsterdam: Elsevier, 770–71.

Schatz, T. 2003. "The Structural Influence: New Directions in Film Genre Studies." In *Film Genre Reader III*, ed. B. K. Grant. University of Texas Press (91–101).

Shklovsky, V. 1965. "Art as Technique." In *Russian Formalist Criticism: Four Essays*, trans. L. T. Lemon and M. J. Reiss. London: University of Nebraska Press (3–24).

Simons, J. 2008. "Complex Narratives." *New Review of Film and Television Studies* 6, no. 2: 111–26.

Smith, G. M. 2004. *Film Structure and the Emotion System*. Cambridge: Cambridge University Press.

Smith, M. 1995. *Engaging Characters: Fiction, Emotion and the Cinema*. Oxford: Oxford University Press.

Sobchack, V. 2000. "At the Still Point of the Turning World." In *Meta-Morphing*. Minnesota: Minnesota University Press (131–58).

Spivack, G., J. J. Platt, and M. B. Shure. 1976. *The Problem-Solving Approach to Adjustment: A Guide to Research and Intervention*. San Francisco: Jossey-Bass.

Sternberg, R. J. 1995. "Expertise in Complex Problem Solving: a Comparison of Alternative Conceptions." In *Complex Problem Solving: The European Perspective*, eds. P. A. Frensch and J. Funke. Hillsdale: Lawrence Erlbaum Associates (295–322).

Stout, C. J. 1999. "Artists as Writers: Enriching Perspectives in Art Appreciation." *Studies in Art Education* 40, no. 3: 226–41.

Tan, E. 1996. *Emotion and the Structure of Narrative Film*. Mahwah: LEA Publishers.

Taylor, G. T. 1992. "The Cognitive Instrument in the Service of Revolutionary Change: Sergei Eisenstein, Annette Michelson, and the Avant-Garde's Scholarly Aspiration." *Cinema Journal* 31, no. 4: 42–59.

Teigen, K. H., and G. Keren. 2003. "Surprises: Low Probabilities or High Contrasts?" *Cognition* 87, no. 2: 55–71. Thomas, R. P., M. R. Dougherty, A. M. Sprenger, and I. Harbison. 2008. "Diagnostic Hypothesis Generation and Human Judgment." *Psychological Review* 115, no. 1: 155–85.

Triantaphyllou, E. 2000. *Multi-criteria Decision Making: A Comparative Study*. Dordrecht: Kluwer Academic Publishers (now Springer).

Tynjanov, Y. 1981. "Foundations of Cinema." In *Russian Formalist Film Theory*, trans. H. Eagle. Michigan: University of Michigan Press (81–100).

Ungar, M. 2001. "Constructing Narratives of Resilience with High-Risk Youth." *Journal of Systemic Therapies* 20, no. 2: 58–73.

Vorderer, P., H. J. Wulff, and M. Friedrichsen, eds. 1996. *Suspense: Conceptualizations, Theoretical Analyses, and Empirical Explorations*. Mahwah: Lawrence Erlbaum Associates.

White, H. 1978. *Tropics of Discourse: Essays in Cultural Criticism.* Baltimore: John Hopkins University Press.

White, M., and M. Epston. 1990. *Narrative Means to Therapeutic Ends.* New York: W. W. Norton and Company.

Winner, E., and L. Hetland. 2001. "Research in Arts Education: Directions for the Future." In *Conference Proceedings from Beyond the Soundbite: What the Research Actually Shows about Arts Education and Academic Outcome*, eds. E. Winner and L. Hetland. Los Angeles: The J. Paul Getty Trust (143–48).

Wulff, H. J. 1996. "Suspense and the Influence of Cataphora on Viewers Expectations." In *Suspense: Conceptualizations, Theoretical Analyses, and Empirical Explorations*, eds. P. Vorderer, H. J. Wulff, and M. Friedrichsen. Mahwah: Lawrence Erlbaum Associates (1–18).

Zajonc, R. B. 1984. "On the Primacy of Affect." *American Psychologist* 39, February: 117–23.

Zillmann, D. 1996. "The Psychology of Suspense in Dramatic Exposition." In *Suspense: Conceptualizations, Theoretical Analyses, and Empirical Explorations*, eds. P. Vorderer, H. J. Wulff, and M. Friedrichsen. Mahwah: Lawrence Erlbaum Associates.

Index

Lightning Source UK Ltd.
Milton Keynes UK
UKOW06f1259140415

249620UK00006B/126/P